House of Healing

www.missamandaksite.wordpr

missamandak44@gmail.com

Copyright © 2023 Amanda Hurd

All rights reserved. This book or any portion thereof may not be reproduced or used in any manner whatsoever without the express written permission of the author, except as permitted by U.S. copyright law.

Although this publication is designed to provide accurate information in regard to the subject matter covered, the publisher and the author assume no responsibility for errors, inaccuracies, omissions, or any other inconsistencies herein. This publication is meant as a source of valuable information for the reader, however it is not meant as a replacement for direct expert assistance. If such a level of assistance is required, the services of a competent professional should be sought.

Printed by DiggyPOD, Inc., in the United States of America.

First printing, 2023

ISBN: 979-8-388-39791-1

All scripture references are taken from the New International Version unless otherwise stated.

Thank you . . .

This book is dedicated to my best friend and favorite person ever - Jesus. Without Him, I'd still be a baby caterpillar, endlessly chewing on my past, my shame and the dream of living free.

Thank you for making me new. Thank you for letting me wrestle, so I could grow wings and fly. This book is for you and because of you Abba.

Acknowledgements

Holy cow, where do I start? The amount of people who poured into me through my journey to recovery is unfathomable. I could spend days recounting all the stories about the people who impacted my life.

I could never name everyone who prayed, encouraged and taught me. So, I will do my best to highlight the ones who had major roles in my recovery or this book.

Ryan Nicholas - My love muffin. You've loved me at my literal worst. You've prayed for me more times than you have hairs on your head. You are a precious gift from God & I am so glad you are my husband.

Stacey Ellertson - You are much more than a counselor to me. I'm so grateful for your friendship & encouragement. You pushed me. You wept with me. You told me the truth over & over (and over) until I believed it. You were the hands God used to pull me out of the pit. Because of you, I have the ability to pull others out of theirs. You were a huge part of this book coming to fruition. Thank you!

Mom & Steve - Thank you for your consistency. When everything in my world fell apart, you two were always there. Having people I could count on made the hardest days easier & the good days brighter.

Angel Martinez - I never wanted someone to have to share the pit with me, but having you in the process made it that much better & more fruitful. Love you twin!

Blair Parke - Thank you for your supreme editing skills & dedication to this project (even through Hurricane Ian). Even though the final product is a bit different than what you worked on, your contribution is seen all throughout these pages.

TABLE OF CONTENTS

Chapter 1:
BRICK BY BRICK

Chapter 2:
YOU HAVE TO CHOOSE

Chapter 3:
THE TRUST FALL

Chapter 4:
EMBRACING THE PROCESS

Chapter 5:
SEEING CLEARLY IN THE DARK

Chapter 6:
SHUT THE DOOR!

Chapter 7:
PRACTICAL TIPS FOR RECOVERY

Chapter 8:
GRACE AND HONEY

Chapter 9:
MASTERING THE MELODIES OF OUR HEARTS

Chapter 10:
LIVING IN THE UNKNOWN

Chapter 1:
BRICK BY BRICK

Anxiety has been a passenger on the journey of my life for as long as I can remember. As a kid, it showed up in small ways. I have a distinct memory of being around ten years old reading a magazine. It was the typical teeny-bopper magazines that were so popular in the 90s. While there was nothing wrong with it as a whole, I remember being terrified after reading an article about someone who died and was buried in a coffin.

What was death like?

Would I be alone when I die?

Was there an afterlife?

All these questions swirled through my head as heavy nausea mixed with panic coursed through my veins. I quickly decided that thinking about those things got me nowhere, so I shook off the icky feelings and moved on. From time to time, that old fear crept up when I saw someone die in a movie. Though the feelings were never persistent and I easily moved past them.

My senior year of high school, I began to have panic attacks even though I had little other experience with anxiety up to that point. The attacks happened off and on for years and were terrifying enough that I sought professional help and ended up on prescription medication for anxiety. Having to be medicated was humiliating and made me feel ashamed of myself. I wasn't sure if my recreational drug use in high school contributed to the problem or if I was just a screwed-up person who would be chained to meds for the rest of my life.

Though I had panic attacks regularly for a while, anxiety wasn't something that completely debilitated me at this point. For the most part, until my thirties, anxiety was an obnoxious "back seat driver" that occasionally tried to take me off course, but never completely detoured my life and plans for the future.

Then 2017 happened.

Going into that year, I thought it would be my best year yet. I survived many personal traumas from the previous year and made changes to get my life on the right track. But many times, when we least expect it, that is the exact moment we end up in a pit. I don't say this to scare you. I'm sharing this with you so that you will read this book with an open mind and allow the Holy Spirit to examine your heart so you can do the work to heal before you get to the place I did. If you are reading this book because you've found yourself in a pit so dark you can't imagine seeing the light again, please don't give up hope. There is a way through and out.

I started this journey out of the pit six years ago. Even though anxiety has lurked in the background most of my life, I never expected to live under its grip every day for six years. Random panic attacks are child's play compared to what it's been like to fight out of this place of chronic fear and torment.

The nagging fear I experienced off and on as a child reared its ugly head in 2017. Though the fear was no longer about death, the new subject matter did little to make it less painful. After speaking in front of one hundred women at church and declaring the goodness of God, I woke up the next day covered in fear. A foreboding sense of doom loomed over me as thoughts about God not being real ravaged my mind.

Why is this happening?

What is wrong with me?

I knew about spiritual warfare, but I had no understanding of how to defend myself when the enemy sucker-punched me. So I caved, I cried and I panicked. For months I lived with racing thoughts about Jesus' death on the cross being a hoax. Then one day in the summer of 2017, I was driving to church and heard a demonic voice speak to me.

BRICK BY BRICK

It sounded as if the spine tingling voice of Lord Voldemort from *Harry Potter* crept over my shoulder and whispered into my ear. Essentially, the demon wanted me dead, but he wanted me to be the one to inflict the pain. When I thought my mental state couldn't get much worse, it did. The months of torment over God not being real turned into years of tormenting thoughts about self-harm, evil thoughts about God, doubt, fear, you name it, I thought it. So, when I tell you I know what it is like to be in the pit, I mean it.

This book is not another self-help guide written by someone who studied "mentally ill" people out of a textbook without any understanding of what it's like to go head to head with evil. This book is years upon years of tears, frustration and pain. This book is my way of serving notice to everyone (and everything) on this planet that fear does not own me. I may have given anxiety a "guest room" in my heart for far too long, but this is the eviction notice. It's not welcome here anymore.

So, are you ready to do the same? While this book primarily focuses on getting out of the pit of anxiety, if your struggle is with depression or trauma, you can learn things from these pages. God wants you healed. He wants you to be whole. Jesus didn't die so we could live as a shell of who He made us to be. That thought alone is what has kept me in this fight for so long.

It is why I didn't quit after two years of therapy didn't "seem" to fix me.

It is why I didn't quit after four years in the pit, when my physical health fell apart and I had to start the healing process all over again.

It's why I didn't quit when there didn't seem to be a doctor on the planet who could get me well and keep me there.

If you feel hopeless, helpless and like you are permanently stuck with a brain and/or body bent on tormenting you, I get it. I lived there for a very long time. I know how hard it is to bare your soul to doctor after doctor, only to see your bank account dwindle more than your symptoms. I know what it feels like to put years of effort into healing only to hear, for the eighteenth thousandth time, "It's a process. You're going to have to be patient."

So, I don't know what you are expecting out of this book but, if anything, it is a gentle, empathetic hand reaching out to you. This book is my way of saying, "God gave me the power to overcome. **He can do the same for you.**" Let me show you how. Let me walk you through all the mistakes I made. Let me help you avoid the pitfalls in mental health recovery. Let my words be a light guiding you up the ladder, one rung at a time, until the pit is behind you and you walk free.

In the Old Testament, the word often used for peace is "shalom." This word is used in Isaiah 53 when it talks about what Jesus's death on the cross did for us. It says, "But he was pierced for our transgressions, he was crushed for our iniquities; the punishment that brought us **peace** was on him, and by his wounds we are healed" (Is 53:5).

The peace it talks about goes far deeper than emotion. That type of peace is best described as total well-being or wholeness. It's said when Jewish people would come to the completion of a building and they put the last stone in place, they brought the building into "shalom."[1] They brought completion or soundness to that structure. Every brick laid, every bit of mud dug through, was all a part of making the beautiful, unique structure standing before them.

So it is with us.

God wants to take you brick by brick, layer by layer through the process of healing until you are whole. He doesn't want you to **experience** healing every now and then. He wants you to **live** in health and wholeness. Jesus came to bring us shalom: not just emotional peace, but peace of the mind, body, soul, and spirit. For this is why He died and rose.

Friend, if you are in a place where you want nothing more than peace that consumes your being, let this book be a sign that it is possible. Don't buy the lie that Jesus died only to give you a promise of experiencing peace one day in heaven. Don't buy the lie that says suffering is your portion in life. Suffering happens; there's no way to deny it. But Jesus didn't die to leave you in a perpetual pit. He died to bring you shalom.

The question is: Are you committed to healing?

This is not a self-help book, but a book where you will have to combine your will and the power of the Spirit to make changes. It doesn't matter if you've already heard everything I am going to tell you. If you're reading this book because you've found yourself in a pit, you will have to move beyond knowing about the truth, to believing and applying it. You will need to do a mental, emotional and physical overhaul.

If you don't commit to doing what you read about in these pages, you might as well not read them. It will be hard. Consider this the beginning of open-heart surgery. You will have to allow God to come in with His supernatural scalpel and remove the things inside that are killing you. That may be belief systems, it may be emotional pain you haven't processed and it may be unhealthy habits you haven't had the courage to let go of.

Please friend, whatever you do, don't delay healing any longer. Commit now to starting the next chapter of this book with a focus on starting a new life. As we journey through each chapter, you will see that I've layered the topics in a strategic way. Each chapter of this book will symbolize a piece that goes into building your "house of healing." At the end, I want you to imagine me putting the blueprints for your "house" into the fully capable hands of the Master Architect. There, brick by brick, layer by layer, you will continue the process of coming into wholeness and peace.

It is time. Your future is worth it. YOU are worth it. If you're ready to find freedom, will you read the simple prayer below and spend a moment talking with Jesus about the new adventure you're taking together? If you don't know Him, flip to page 111 for information on what it's like being the son or daughter of the

Most High King. Pray this with me:

Father,

I've been hurting for a long time. I've dealt with (Insert every hurt, pain and point of frustration you need healing in) for way too long. God, I know that You do not put anxiety and depression on me because both issues are often rooted in lies. You are not a man that You should lie (Num 23:19). You would never push me to fear. You have not given me a spirit of fear (2 Tim 1:7). You would never belittle and berate me. I was bought with a price (1 Cor 7:23). I am adopted into a royal family and there is no condemnation for those in Christ (Rom 8:1).

Help me believe these things. Root these truths into the deepest parts of my mind, heart, soul and spirit until I live as the new creation You died to make me. Father, rid me of (insert your particular issues, whether they be anxiety, depression, anger, unforgiveness, trauma, doubt, etc). Pull out every thought, belief and heart posture that sets itself up against Your truth. Show me where the enemy is masquerading himself in my mind as an angel of light (2 Cor 11:14). Light up my dark thoughts and show me the true light. Give me grace and confidence in believing how much You love me. Give me hope to believe whom the Son sets free is free indeed!

Amen

Chapter 2:
YOU HAVE TO CHOOSE

The first step of my journey toward healing was learning how to take control of my thoughts. We will talk more in-depth about spiritual warfare, emotions and nutrition in later chapters because before we do anything, we need to understand how the mind/brain works. This is the most crucial and foundational step of the healing process, which is why I put it in the first chapter.

Without a real understanding that **you control** your thoughts and **they don't control** you, everything else we talk about won't matter. Is it important to discuss trust in God, emotional honesty and spiritual warfare? Yes. But if you don't believe you have the power to think differently than you do now, then reading the following chapters will be all for nothing. Why spend the time reading if you don't have the ability to apply it, right?

As I briefly mentioned in the previous chapter, this skill is not something I was, ahem, born with. My natural tendency was so bent towards being afraid of myself and my thoughts, I could've put the Cowardly Lion out of business. I failed at taking control of my thoughts for a really, really long time. The fact that I am writing a book and teaching people how to do that is nothing short of miraculous (and a little bit funny). But that is how God works, am I right?

Now that you are aware of how hard this skill was for me to learn, I want you to take a deep breath. Before you go any further into this chapter, I need you to inhale a huge breath of grace and release any expectations for what this will look like for you. You may master taking control of your thoughts in a few months. For some of you, it may take a while longer. Either is OK. Neither way is failing. The only way you fail is to let your thoughts take over and make no effort to fight back.

If you are trying, even if you don't see obvious progress, you are moving forward. Please get that settled in your mind right now. Progress is happening every single day you choose to apply the things you read in this book, especially if you are pairing them with what you learn in the word of God. You can not be stuck when you partner with Jesus. Whew! I say those words knowing some of you don't believe that right now. I say those words knowing how long I didn't believe that. So, move aside all expectations and let the process begin.

To start, I want to show you how the body and brain work together so you can understand the root of most anxiety, which is stress. Stress chemicals adrenaline, cortisol and norepinephrine, are not inherently bad.[2] We need them in times of danger to increase our rate of thinking and heighten our senses. However, when we get into a chronically stressed state that can be referred to as stress hyperstimulation, that is where the problems come in. Stress hyperstimulation is what happens when the stress response in the body is activated repeatedly and doesn't have enough time to properly allow the body to recover afterwards.[2] While the rules of how stress is created apply to every person reading this book, every person struggling with anxiety may not get to a point of hyperstimulation.

Though, even if you think you have "high-functioning anxiety," learning about how stress affects the body/brain is important so you don't move from "high-functioning" to hyperstimulated. I have found that many people don't do well with admitting how stressed/anxious they are. Whether the stress comes from taking on more than they should, toxic relationships they don't want to leave or being afraid of their thoughts, most people deny stress/anxiety is at the root of why they can't sleep, can't eat and feel jittery all the time. Maybe you've said things like:

"I'm not anxious. I just drank too much coffee."

"I'm not stressed! I can handle it. I don't need help."

"I sleep enough. I may toss and turn for an hour or two, but four to five hours of sleep is all I need."

If any of those statements sound vaguely familiar, may I be the first to say, you might have an issue with stress/anxiety. Outside

YOU HAVE TO CHOOSE

of underlying health issues, having insomnia, digestive problems, jitters and so on are cues that your body is under stress. Never allowing others to help is also a sure fire way to reach your stress limit. So, even if it's uncomfortable to think of yourself as an "anxious person," continue through this chapter with me and consider what habits may be leading you into more stress/anxiety than you realize.

Years ago, my counselor shared an analogy about stress that illuminated how it works in the body. He said each of us has a "cup" inside our body. That cup represents the amount of stress we can hold. Each person's cup is different and we have no control over how much ours holds. The key to making sure your cup doesn't get full and spill over is not figuring out the exact amount of stress you can hold so you can push yourself to the max. But that is exactly what we would do if we had that kind of information, right?

Humans, Americans in particular, hate to slow down. We hate having to admit we can't do everything on our own. We hate realizing we are fragile, limited beings. Though, if you want to heal and live a life of peace, accepting your limitations is crucial. There is no way to live a stress-free life on planet earth. It just isn't possible. So, the next best thing we can do to live healthy, productive lives is figure out how to manage the stress we do have and admit when we need to pull back and make changes so our "cup" doesn't spill over.

The key to managing stress is learning how your body responds to stress naturally and things you can do to reduce stress. There are several ways we can create stress in our bodies. One major stressor is not getting adequate sleep. Carrying the weight of toxic relationships also contributes to stress. A poor diet including too much caffeine, alcohol or sugar will also throw your body into a frazzled state.

Managing these things is very important because these variables alone are enough to create stress hyperstimulation in your body. **Since anxiety symptoms are symptoms of stress,** if you have symptoms of anxiety in your body and brain, you need to take a long look at the relationships, habits and/or nutrition that may be causing you stress.

Thankfully, if a lack of sleep is the only thing causing your body stress and there are no underlying health conditions keeping you from sleeping, you can make simple adjustments and feel better within a few weeks to a month. The average amount of sleep needed per night is debated, though it is generally thought to be ideal to get between seven to eight hours of sleep each night.[3] Making sure you get enough rest will play a big role in your recovery. So, please don't overlook this simple step as a part of the process.

We will discuss the specifics of caffeine, alcohol and sugar consumption later in the book. As a general rule, you do not need to have all three every day. Our bodies are strong and resilient machines, but we can not overwhelm them with chemicals and expect to live in optimal health. If you are at a point where you feel like you can't make it through the day without caffeine, alcohol or sugar then you may have some underlying emotional/physical issues that need to be addressed so you can get yourself into a more peaceful state. While hyperstimulation due to poor sleep patterns or even diet can be solved relatively quickly, the reason it is often so hard to get your body out of a hyperstimulated state is that most people end up there **because of the way they think.**

Being stressed because of lack of sleep, poor diet, or stressful relationships does the exact same thing to your body physically as negative thinking. But if you deal with relationship stressors and eating habits and still have anxiety issues, your problem is likely in your thought life. Like I said before, when we get stressed, no matter the cause, our body produces the stress hormones cortisol, adrenaline and norepinephrine.[2] These stress hormones are leaked into our bloodstream and pushed to different places in the body to bring physiological, psychological and emotional changes.

YOU HAVE TO CHOOSE

You have probably heard of the "fight-or-flight response" coming over people when they get stuck in a tough situation. This is the exact same thing as a stress response; this is our body's way of responding to a threat to help us stay safe. If the stress response is engaged every now and then, and relieved with good rest and nutrition, you won't notice prolonged changes to your body or brain. However, if you are afraid of your thoughts and feelings or there's something else that is repetitively causing you stress, that is how you end up in stress hyperstimulation.

If you get stuck on a disturbing thought and panic everytime it comes to mind, this triggers the stress response over and over. That response can make you feel like you need to go into "fight" mode. If you are being chased by a wild animal, a repetitive thought focused on the animal and loads of adrenaline is helpful. But when the stress response is activated and you start fighting against yourself, you can see how quickly the situation can turn from helpful to harmful.

The interesting thing about the brain is it can not tell the difference between a perceived threat and an actual threat. For example, if you think about paying bills and always worry if you will pay them on time, you tell your brain that thoughts about paying bills are threatening. So, it takes note of that and will keep bringing it back up until you decide that it is no longer a "threat."

Your brain doesn't know if you have the money in your bank account or not. All it knows is that the thought bothers you. So, in this situation, even if you cut back on caffeine, sugar and get good rest, but don't learn to extinguish your fear of not having money to pay the bills, you will stay stressed. **Thinking apprehensively is enough to keep the body in stress hyperstimulation.** To overcome anxiety, that is the first step you have to master.

As you read in the intro, I got to a place where I was so overstimulated, dark thoughts peppered me night and day like a spastic lawn sprinkler. It was never-ending and no matter what I did, they only seemed to get more disturbing. I thought I was losing my mind. It made no sense why my thoughts would not shut up and quit going to this dark place. This was due, in part, to stress hyperstimulation. I was terrified of my own thoughts, so I stayed in a perpetual state of stress.

When we get hyperstimulated, our brains also generate more thoughts with a more disturbing tone. Your thoughts are made to race so you notice them and can either deal with a real threat that's in front of you or deal with the things you are stressed about. If you notice the thoughts taking a weirder or more ominous turn, that happens because your brain is scanning for danger. Though it will feel like you are going crazy, it is just your brain creating as many thoughts, and variations of those thoughts, to assess every possible danger there might be.

The stress response also increases activity in the emotional part of your brain and lowers activity in the rational part. The idea is that if something is actually threatening you, you don't need to sit around trying to rationalize how to deal with it. You need to think fast and "get the heck out of dodge" as us Southerns like to say. So, once you establish a threat in your brain, it increases thought production and awareness of danger, as well as restricting rationale so you can be hyper aware of the problem.

If the threat is eliminated quickly, you should feel calmer within the hour. However, if you keep ruminating on an issue and overstimulating yourself, you can expect to get yourself weaved into a web of chronic, obsessive thinking. Thinking in an anxious way stimulates the stress hormones to deal with the problem. Those hormones bring on more thoughts and feelings of fear, and if you don't know what to do with them, they will reactivate the response all over again and the cycle continues until you learn how to stop it.

If you don't know any of the things I just told you, don't feel bad; I didn't either. It's understandable if you have believed you are crazy up to this point, but that thought process has to change. When you get yourself into a hyperstimulated state and your brain is creating thoughts at a rapid fire pace, with an increasingly scary tone, it's natural to think something is wrong.

YOU HAVE TO CHOOSE

Who wouldn't? But instead of asking, "What's wrong with me?" or "Am I losing my mind?," the better question may be, "How can I take control of my thoughts?"

If you'll look back over everything I've said in this chapter, you'll notice that I used the word brain repetitively, not mind.

Our **brains** can not tell the difference between a perceived threat and a real threat.

Our **brains** are flooded with stress chemicals that excite the emotional center and constrict the rational portion.

Our **brains** bring up a threat over and over until it is extinguished.

So, how do we extinguish our fears if the organ that should lead our whole body is the one flooded with fear chemicals, spinning us in circles of anxious thoughts?

We do that . . . with our **minds**. Our minds are completely separate from our brains. Our minds are part of our spirits and / or souls. I've debated over whether it is actually in the spirit or the soul and haven't come to a conclusion. Yet, I do know that our minds are the intangible pieces of our beings that sit inside our bodies, observe our thoughts and give us the ability to choose. If you need some help understanding this, walk through an exercise with me.

Get still and quiet. Turn off the music. Turn off your TV. Turn off all noise around you. Now, observe the thoughts that flow through your brain. There may be a few; there may be a dozen. How many there are doesn't matter. Just sit still and observe them. Notice that many of them are not coming from you intentionally thinking of them; they randomly pop into your brain.

Now, I want you to purposefully think about your next meal. What will you eat? Think of two options. Which one will be more fattening? Which one will taste better? Pick one and think about why that's a better option. Then think about the other one and

~ 13 ~

why that might be the better option. Now decide on one, but don't go to the kitchen yet.

Notice that while these thoughts were spinning around in your brain, you had the ability to observe them. You heard them inside your head as if you were a bystander listening in on someone else's conversation. You may have seen visuals pop up as they strolled through. But never once did they force you to do anything. They didn't jump out of your brain, shove you into the kitchen and make you make a sandwich. You decided to think about them, picked the best option for food and/or pushed it off until later.

You decided. How did you do that? Your mind.

Your mind is the invisible observer of your being. Your mind is how you sit back, observe your thoughts and make decisions in the middle of one thousand possibilities swirling through your brain. If all you had was a brain housing ideas, with nothing to observe and decide, none of what just happened would be possible. Your mind is not the same as your brain, and that is great news for anyone caught in the throes of anxiety or depression.

You may think you are going nuts and can't control your thoughts.

You may think staying in bed is the only way to deal with sadness.

You may think a lot of things, but you always have a choice to do something different than what you think or feel. That is thanks to your mind. On her podcast, Dr. Caroline Leaf, a cognitive neuroscientist, said this about the brain/mind connection:

> "The mind works through the brain. The brain does not produce the mind. We are often told the brain produces the mind, but that is incorrect. The mind works through the brain and the brain responds to the mind. Your brain can't do anything without YOU. Your brain can't do anything that you don't tell it to do. What you tell your brain to do, it then tells your body to do."[4]

YOU HAVE TO CHOOSE

Later in the show she said:

> "The world tells us we are preprogrammed and the result of our genes, i.e. we are robots. But we are brilliant, deep thinking, human beings with the ability to choose and when we choose, we influence the physical nature of how we function."[4]

We don't always have control over what thought pops into our heads. As we saw in the experiment earlier, random thoughts pop up from time to time. We don't have control over what was passed down through our genetics. We don't have control over what bad behaviors we were taught or learned growing up. **What we can control is how we think and respond to all of that.**

Dr. Leaf has also stated that research shows the way we think affects our mental (and physical) health by a factor of 75% - 98%.[4] So, even if you were born into an anxiety ridden family, you don't have to stay that way. You have a mind and you can use it to think differently. You used your mind to decide to pick up this book. Something told you the information in these pages might help you. You used your mind to move the book from a shelf to your hands. You used your mind every time you chose to turn a page instead of putting it down to scroll on your phone. You chose. You decided. You have power in this fight. This chapter and this book is all about teaching you how to unlock that power and walk in the authority God has given you!

While we are on the subject of choosing what we believe, I want to ask you not **what** do you believe, but **who** do you believe? Some of the things written in this book are counter-cultural. I believe that demons are real and try to have influence in the life of every human on earth. I believe we have control over our brains and the way we think and we are not slaves to our genetics and/or neurotransmitter levels. I believe forgiveness is a necessary step towards healing. I believe all these things because the Bible tells me they are true.

Thankfully, as I showed you earlier, we have scientific research that backs up our ability to lead our thoughts with our mind.

However, there are still people in the medical community who refuse to acknowledge that fact. The foundational belief of Western medicine is that all mental health issues are rooted in chemical imbalances or faulty genetics. We are victims they say, nothing more, nothing less. There is nothing we can do about the "cards we were dealt in life."

By the grace of the pharmaceutical gods alone, in the last thirty or so years, some say we have advanced beyond the "dark ages" of believing demonic presences could have a role in mental health issues. We are turning less and less to spiritual implications or mind renewal as a source of healing the mind, body, soul and spirit. Simply put, pills are it.

Pills, Pills, Pills. Can you get me some more of those pills? It's like Big Pharma spent the last thirty years rewriting Destiny Child's iconic song, "Bills Bills Bills" into their own personal anthem, but I digress. Some days I relate to Alice from Wonderland when she said, "Nothing would be what it is, because everything would be what it isn't. And contrariwise, what it is, it wouldn't be, and what it wouldn't be, it would. You see?"

It's all backwards. Our world is flipped upside down and inside out. Right is called wrong and left is called right. So, the question remains, **who** will you believe? It's impossible for you to walk in the fullness of freedom that Jesus died to give you without deciding who you believe, because knowing and living in the truth is what Jesus promised would set us free (John 8:32).

In our backwards, upside down world where the people who are supposed to help us, support ideas that lead us into victimhood, so their pockets can grow faster than my waistline after Thanksgiving, it's hard to trust that a God you can't see will be any different. By no means do I want to put down the entire medical community as a whole.

I have several family members and friends who are doctors and nurses and I highly respect them. However, I do find much of Western medicine's ideology to be at odds with what the Bible teaches and with giving treatment that heals people rather than enslaves them to a pharmaceutical master.

While I don't think all pills or doctors are evil, I do think you will have to decide where your allegiance is before going forward. For example, if a doctor tells you that you are stuck in this pit of anxiety because you grew up in a family that also struggle with it, but God's word says you can be transformed by the renewing of your mind (Rom 12:2), who will you believe? If people tell you that you are crazy for believing in demonic spirits, but you know, like I know, when something otherworldly speaks to you, who will you believe? If someone tells you that the key to getting over trauma is getting revenge, but the Bible says you should forgive those who hurt you (Matt 6:14), who will you believe?

I understand if you aren't at a place where you're ready to throw your very real and very breakable heart into the hands of an invisible God. It's scary. It takes time to trust. We will spend the entire next chapter talking about that very thing. But I do want you to ponder a few questions before we wrap up this chapter:

- What holds you back from trusting Jesus is exactly who He says He is? (Heb 13:5, John 14:18, Ps 86:15, John 8:36)

- Do people or God's word have a heavier influence on how you think?

- Are you ready to go against what the world says if God's word tells you it's true and could bring healing?

We all have a choice. Actually, we have millions of choices we make each day. Every single one of them matters. We are either walking towards healing or away from it. While we have to take control of our thoughts, we have to choose to allow God in the process too. To continue in your journey toward healing, you will have to open your heart to Him. He is Jehovah Rapha (Ex 15:26). He promises to be the God who heals us.

So, even if you aren't sure about God, even if people have hurt you so badly you believe there's a snowball's chance in July that Jesus could be any different, even if you think you are stuck in a perpetual pit of pain, will you give this a chance anyways? Will you open your heart and mind to the idea that there is a God who loves you and is wildly different from the chaos we see on earth and in the people who live here? Will you dip one tiny toe into the pool of possibility and ask Jesus to help you see that He wants to heal you? Pray this prayer with me:

Father,

It's time for me to make a choice. To be honest, I'm scared. I'm scared that this will be another failed attempt to get my life back. I'm scared that I may waste more time chasing another "cure" that doesn't work. I'm scared that You may not really love me (or insert whatever fear/doubt you have).

I need You to show me that I can trust You. I need to see Your truth with my own eyes. Help me to see it, Jesus. I want to be free. Your Word says that I can be free (John 8:36, Rom 8:2, Gal 5). God show me how to get there. Help me take the steps I need to take to walk in peace and wholeness. Use this book to speak to me directly and specifically. God show me the power that raised Jesus from the dead that is available to me and can put the pieces of my broken life back together.

Amen

Chapter 3:
THE TRUST FALL

I think equally as important as knowing if God is real, is knowing that God is good and can be trusted. The only thing worse than living in a Godless universe would be living with a God bent on torturing His subjects. Part of building your house of healing will include learning to trust and depend on the character of God.

Whether or not you know this, what you believe about God matters. What you think about His existence or lack thereof shapes everything you do in life. Now, there will be atheists/agnostics that swear that they want nothing to do with "religion" and would rather keep any trace of supernatural influence away from them. Even though they may not realize it, the view they have about the spirit world shapes how they live. If you don't believe Jesus is Lord and think you are instead, you will live by your own code of morality instead of the guidelines of God's heart. His heart dictates that we love Him and others above ourselves. If we all adopted this mindset, every need each of us has would be taken care of by someone else.

Yet, we see so much pain and suffering in the world and we wonder why? Why would a "good" God allow all of this to happen? Why does a "good" God let people starve to death? Why does a "good" God let people rob, kill and cheat? While it isn't wrong to wonder about these things, I think we can get stuck if we stop there. If we are going to ask those questions, we also need to ask, "What does God's word say about such things?"

You don't have to go far in the Bible to see that a) there is a supernatural war going on between God, man and our adversary the devil, b) man has a choice and c) our choices often don't mirror the choices God would like for us to make. Within the first four chapters of Genesis, God makes man, gives man authority over the earth and we end up with brokenness and death. God tells Adam and Eve to not eat from the tree of the knowledge of good and evil. God gave them a garden full of good things to eat and look at and the only thing He asked was that they never make the choice to know what evil is like. What a request!

Yet, their curiosity and pride lead them to bring thousands of years worth of hurt upon the world. Not long after they are kicked out of the garden for their bad choices, we see their son Cain murder his brother. This comes shortly after God warns him that sin crouches at the "door" and he must rule over it (Gen 4:7). Murder, sin, pain and heartache, four chapters into the great history of the world and we are drowning in sorrow. Where did it all go wrong? Better yet, how did this great God, who painted the sky with the cadence of His sovereign voice, lose control of the entire world? Why did He let His perfect creation get destroyed so easily?

Within the answer to that question lies one of the most heartbreaking, yet utterly beautiful rules of the universe we live in: free will. God gave us the ability to choose. As I mentioned in the last chapter, the Bible says we don't have to conform to the ways of this world, but we can choose to trust God's word and think differently because of it (Rom 12). The problem is that we often choose not to. Sin crouches at our door and much like Cain we invite it in, have a party and make friends with it, instead of ruling over it.

While we all might wonder if God lost His sovereign mind when He gave sin-prone creatures the ability to choose, He didn't. God isn't any more crazy for giving us free will than He is for allowing us to co-labor in the future of the world with Him. God is love and love requires that it not be forced or manipulated. 1 Corinthians 13 says:

> "Love is patient, love is kind. It does not envy, it does not boast, it is not proud. It does not dishonor others, it is not self-seeking, it is not easily angered, it keeps no record of wrongs. Love does not delight in evil but rejoices with the truth. It always protects, always trusts, always hopes, always perseveres."

God's love always brings us into relationship. His desire for us to partner with Him is where we get the phrase "co-laboring." This idea can be found in Genesis 2 when the Father, Son and Spirit are seen together speaking as a trio about making man in their image and giving the freedom to rule over the earth they just created. Our undeniable place on this earth is not only co-laboring and caring for the earth with God, but also co-reigning and ruling over the earth with God!

We have an incredible responsibility to take care of the world God gave us, yet I am sure each person reading this book has at some point been the victim of behavior that doesn't live up to God's royal standards of love. So again, we end up asking, "Why does God let this happen?" His word clearly shows us that He sets out rules of love for us to live by. He intends for us to live in the peace-filled, harmonious world He envisioned when He placed Adam and Eve in the Garden of Eden. So, when we see breeches in the perfect plan God made, what we must never do is look at Him with a heart of accusation and contempt. **Sin was not God's idea.** Pain and suffering are not God's will.

People will sometimes suggest that because God is sovereign, He is ultimately in charge of all our decision making. That couldn't be further from the truth. Yes, God knows what is going to happen, but He forces no one to do anything. He works within the evil world system we created by disobeying Him. But He certainly does not empower us to hurt others, by letting us choose things that go against His word.

Getting an understanding of our ability to choose and God's heart for the human race is critical if we are going to learn to live in peace. You may think I've gone off on a theological tangent, but all of this is the framework for the house we are building that will ultimately be the shelter of hope and healing you reside under in the days to come. Trusting God is of the utmost importance because He is the one who is going to heal us. While therapy is important and proper nutrition is vital, both of those things exist because we serve a God who created foods with healing properties and created people to co-labor with Him in the healing process. So, even though those things are great, let's not forget that God is the source and we need Him.

House of Healing

Even though I've been a Christian most of my life, I also spent a lot of time running from God. I know exactly what it is like to want love so badly, but to not know how to do anything but break God's royal laws of love. As a kid I went through some pretty traumatic things that led me to believe I was worthless, unloveable and crazy. I spent over a decade drinking heavily, experimenting with drugs and allowing myself to get in relationships I knew I had no business being in.

I knew what God's word said. I knew getting black out drunk every weekend was wrong. I knew clinging to ungodly men who didn't love me was not God's best for me. I went to church off and on during that time but continued down my path of self sabotage until my run in with Lord Voldemort in 2017. I lived with a heavy sense of guilt, mixed in with the pleasure my flesh felt indulging in things that helped me forget the pain. The problem wasn't that I didn't know right from wrong. I knew God didn't like the way I was living, but what I didn't know was that **He was the only one who could set me free from it.**

I didn't know the condemnation I heard every time I walked into church was not the voice of my heavenly Father, but the voice of the enemy of my soul. I didn't know that God's kindness draws us to repentance (Rom 2:4). For years I wondered where He was or why I felt so stuck in my bad decisions. Yet, God was there all along. In His kindness, He let me run from Him. In His kindness, He continued wooing me as I ran. And in His kindness, He let the weight of all my bad behavior and trauma come crashing down on me in 2017 so for the first time, I would sit with Him in my heartbreak instead of run from it.

Learning to trust God and live in peace because of that trust has hands down been the hardest thing I have ever done. It has taken me years to learn I am loved, I am not crazy because disturbing thoughts pop up in my brain and no matter how painful life is, God can be trusted to bring good out of every bit of it. If we want to learn to live in peace and begin building a house of healing, then we need to look no further than the book of Isaiah to see why trust is so important in finding peace.

THE TRUST FALL

In Isaiah 26:3 it says, "You will keep in perfect peace those whose minds are steadfast, because they trust in you." In this spiritual recipe for peace we see the first ingredient listed as a mind that is steadfast, i.e. rested and supported by God. If you're like me and every other Millennial kid in America, by age ten you probably witnessed or did a "trust fall" with your friends. This team building exercise is the perfect way to understand how a steadfast mind and trust build the exact formula we need to create peace.

In a trust fall, the person doing the experiment stands with their back to a group of two to three people. The people, hopefully, have their arms out waiting for the lucky "trust faller" to lean backwards and be caught. The person falling has to put their full trust in their friends because they can't see what is behind them. They don't know if someone might sneeze at the last minute as their body is hurling towards the floor. They don't know if their friend may have an underlying resentment for something they did five years ago and decide to move out of the way at the last minute. Since anything can happen from the time you lean backwards until the time your back slams into the forearms of your three best friends, you just have to trust.

This is very similar to how we have to rely on God in our thought life.

Isaiah describes peace coming from a mind supported by God. Essentially, He is saying, once you've done the trust fall with The Lord, by throwing the weight of your world view and self perception upon His word, and you are comfortably resting your mind upon His promises, you will know peace. Peace is a by-product of living by the Spirit of God (Gal 5:22). Jesus Himself said, "Whoever follows me will never walk in darkness, but will have the light of life" (John 8:12).

Getting to the place where you are ready to fling your mind and heart into the hands of God is hard.

You may wonder, *How do I know that when I reveal my secrets to Him, He won't condemn me and send me away from His presence?*

House of Healing

How do I know that He actually loves me?

How can I trust that when I fall into His arms and give Him my entire life, and not just an hour on Sunday, I won't be crushed under the weight of being called a "Jesus freak?"

This is why the verse says you have a "steadfast mind **because** you trust in Him." You won't fling your heart into the arms of God if He doesn't appear to be trustworthy. But, you won't know He is trustworthy until you give Him a chance to show you He can be. You will have to get into God's word and be willing to have it unlock the places you are hiding from Him. Spiritual peace doesn't operate like the RX labeled peace the world offers (John 4:27).

While a trust fall happens in a matter of seconds, trust in God develops moment by moment that you are willing to risk opening up to Him. Over time, you'll notice each small act of faith and encounter with God lays another brick in the foundation of your house of healing. The greater the risk you take with Him, the stronger the foundation is built when He comes through. Then one day, you'll wake up so supported by that foundation, it will feel as if nothing or no one could ever tear you down again.

Because I like to keep a balanced approach in my theology, I don't want to leave that last sentence lingering with the possibility of an unreasonable expectation forming. While the love of Christ is awe inspiring, everyday you are in relationship with Him will not feel like the final scene of a Disney movie. Sorry to be the bearer of bad news, but that is not real life.

I say that because I truly used to believe that people who knew they were loved by God felt like they were walking among the clouds every day of their life. While I have had some experiences with God that left me feeling like I was among the angels themselves, I've also had times where I struggled to feel His presence at all. That is just the way life on planet Earth is. We go through mountain top seasons and we go through valleys. We go through waves of joy and waves of sorrow. If you are going to learn to trust God, one thing I must do is help you have reasonable expectations for what life with Him will be like.

When I first went into counseling in 2018, I believed I was the most unlovable person on the planet. I was disgusted with everything about myself. I didn't like who I had been and I certainly didn't like the panic stricken woman I had become. Nothing about me was good in my eyes. Yet, I kept hearing my counselor tell me, "God loves you."

God loves me, really?, I wondered. *Well if He loves me then why don't I feel it? Why am I not dancing around with a song in my heart and a gleam in my eye?* Because one of my core misbeliefs was that something was wrong with me, it took me a while to grasp that the answer to the question was pretty simple.

There was nothing wrong with me. God loves me, I just don't feel it all the time; neither will you. Being in a relationship with God is similar to a relationship with people in the sense that some days are harder than others. Some days you won't connect the way you expect. Some days you will find great joy in the simplest things being shared. Other days, you may wonder if He has completely forgotten you. This is the nature of relationships on planet earth because emotions are real, confusing and navigating communication in the midst of unruly feelings can be tough.

Though, the one thing that set me free from constantly feeling unloved was realizing that I don't have to **feel** loved every day to **believe** that I am. It's just that simple. We walk by faith and not by sight (2 Cor 5:7). So, if we want to make a step forward in our healing and relationship with God, one thing we must do is accept that we won't feel "butterflies" all the time. When you are going through recovery from anxiety or depression, there will be many days you won't feel the presence of God at all. You will have to choose to walk by faith and believe He is there and He loves you; even though every feeling in your body is agonizing and every thought in your head is anything but loving.

In addition to not relying on your feelings to define the truth, you also will have to face your feelings and not avoid the truth. We have to look our memories in the eye, hand in hand with the Lord, and declare what happened to us will not define us for the rest of our lives. We have to take a bold step towards God and choose to believe that He is good, even if people on earth are not. We have to choose to not engage with thoughts/feelings of self-protection that tell us to run, hide and avoid anything that could bring the trauma to the surface.

If you want to be healed, **you will have to give God a chance to be different from the people who broke your heart**. The person who hurt you, the trauma you face, everything you went through that brought you to the pit will claw at your already fragile heart and beg you to back away from the process of healing. Healing is a bold move because it requires us to put our future into the hands of a God some of us believe may not be worthy to hold it.

If I can promise you one thing, it's this; God is not the same as the people who hurt you. Though, you can read through the hundreds of laws in the Old Testament if you still need some convincing. Outside of spending the next year eyeballs deep in the Torah, you could also look at the commandments that Jesus said stood above them all. In Mark 12, Jesus told a teacher of the law that the most important commands were, "Love the Lord your God with all your heart and with all your soul and with all your mind and with all your strength and love your neighbor as yourself."

At the top of the list, above everything except the love of God Himself, Jesus said loving people is of the utmost importance. It's critical that we get the weight of this statement. The Old Testament laws and New Testament teachings lay out how we are supposed to treat each other with respect, honor and integrity. So, when someone violates those principles we can know with certainty that behavior came from temptation of the devil, their flesh or a combination of both.

It did not and would not ever come from God.

THE TRUST FALL

God's highest aim is that we live in His laws of love, because He is love itself. You are safe in His arms. You can trust Him. He has your back and wants to walk you out of this pit and into a life of freedom. God loves you. Hear that today and choose to disregard any other feeling or thought that might come against it. Invite God into your heart right now. Open it up to Him and let Him prove to you that He is trustworthy and good. Say this prayer with me:

Father,

I want to trust You. I think You could love me, but there are so many things holding me back from fully believing that. Show me who You are. Show me the difference between Your heart and everyone else's. Give me wisdom to know who I can trust and who I can't.

Give me courage to fling my heart into Your hands and let You carry me through this process. God, I need You. I can't get out of this pit alone. I got myself in here, but You have to get me out; show me the way. Continue revealing the hidden things in my heart that are keeping me stuck. Heal me with Your glorious light of life!

Amen

Chapter 9:
EMBRACING THE PROCESS

Now that we've laid a good foundation in our house of healing through learning we have authority over our thoughts/feelings, dug deep into the heart of God and are learning to trust Him, it's time to begin building the walls of our house up. The next step on our journey is learning to trust the process. This concept has been such a thorn in my side, I used to get a twitch every time I heard someone say healing was a "process." Even though I say that as a joke (kind of), I get it if the last thing you want to hear about right now is another lengthy process.

Trusting the process encapsulates so many things you will learn and master as we go through this book. The process includes leaning on the heart of God and trusting Him to heal you. It includes forgiving when you don't feel like it. It includes changing the way you think, eat and live on a daily basis. The process is essentially changing everything about who you are and trusting that with the right work and the power of the Spirit, you will come out on the other side better than ever.

Two years into my battle with anxiety, I had had more people "lay hands on me" for prayer than a heifer prime for milking. I tried several anxiety medications and counselors, but nothing seemed to help. It was especially challenging because I was a newlywed, crying every single day of what should've been our "honeymoon phase." Needless to say, our actual honeymoon and the first two years of our marriage were anything but pleasant. My husband was at a loss for how to "fix me."

I wondered if I would ever look in the mirror and see a woman without bags under her eyes and fear coursing through her veins. I didn't recognize myself anymore. While I didn't like the broken woman I was before, this new version of me was way worse. This is not who I hoped to become.

After two years of living with the chaos in my mind, I met a counselor who labeled my issue as an anxiety disorder. After some

EMBRACING THE PROCESS

conversation, we realized I had several misbeliefs about myself, God and life in general. It would take work - a lot of work - to get me well, but the counselor believed I could do it. The problem was, he thought it would take at least two years before I was fully recovered. Ouch!

Around this same time, a well-meaning friend said, "Look, if you go to a counselor and you aren't 'fixed' in six months, you're seeing the wrong guy." On the surface, it seemed to make sense. Why should healing take so long? Why shouldn't I have a dozen conversations with a counselor and move on? Unfortunately, we live in a super-sonic society. We expect everything to happen in an instant. Let me be clear: **you can not unravel decades of pain and misbeliefs in a matter of months.** It just won't happen.

Some symptoms of depression or anxiety may alleviate after a few months of counseling. It is possible. Though I don't know your story or your circumstances, I do know that when you get to the state of anxiety I was in, it can take years. I set this expectation here for you, so you can relieve yourself of shame. If you have gone from counselor to counselor, recovery practice to recovery practice and months later you don't seem any better off than when you started, it's OK. It takes time, way more than most of us expect. Thankfully, I didn't listen to the advice of my friend. He was one hundred percent wrong.

The counselor I met with at the Anxiety Centre was the only person able to help me. I'm so glad I stuck with him long enough to learn the skills I needed to learn how to live free. Part of what he taught me we already discussed in the chapter on stress hyperstimulation. The other pieces we will discuss in later chapters. For now, I want to hand you a bucket full of grace, in hopes that you will dump it over your head and let it refresh your soul, like cool water on a steamy, summer day.

Because the process of recovery can be grueling, you will need to hold onto this bucket. You'll also need to grab a few more and hand them out to family members. You and everyone you love will need to be doused in grace as you are fighting for your

House of Healing

healing. You will have to let go of your expectations for how it "should feel" and when you "should be" free. Heaping shame for not recovering in a certain amount of time only adds pressure to an already crushed spirit.

Proverbs 16:24 says, "Gracious words are a honeycomb, sweet to the soul and healing to the bones." Gracious words are exactly what you will need to give yourself and encourage your family to give you during the process. As hard as it may be, try to open up with them about how hard it is for you. They may be the type of people that say, "Just get over it" or "Just stop worrying." Don't let that deter you from being vulnerable with them.

Tell them the shame you feel for not being able to "fix yourself" in an instant.

Tell them how scary it is to be stuck in a pit so dark you couldn't see a ladder if there was one.

Tell them the truth — that you realize having an anxious mind makes you afraid of things you know you should not be afraid of. (Ahem . . . your own thoughts).

Tell them how hard it is to feel unrelenting sadness when you already know "you have so much to be grateful for."

You will have to set the expectations for them. **If they haven't lived it, they will have no clue how to help you live through it.**

In the beginning, I was so desperate for help I told everyone about my problems. I felt like I was bleeding out and desperate to find anyone who could bandage the wound. As time went on and I felt like I should be beyond this by now, I started doubting if I would ever live without fear again. Threads of resignation began to weave into my defeated heart. I felt ashamed for sharing the same problem over and over with people. So, I hid it. I tried to not talk about it unless I was on the verge of tears and couldn't hold back any longer.

No one seemed to know what to do, so why drag them through the mud with me, right?

No, friend. Let them walk with you. The body of Christ is designed to carry one another's burdens. While we don't have the power to heal each other in and of ourselves, we have the power to petition heaven on behalf of our friends. There were some powerful times when I opened up to people and let them pray for me that the anxiety lifted instantly. Oftentimes it stayed gone for the rest of the day. If I had stayed clammed up in shame, I would've been robbed of some much needed moments of peace.

Your family and friends may not get it. They may not be able to empathize with you in the way you want them to. That doesn't mean you need to give up on letting others help you. It doesn't mean you need to carry this burden on your own. It also doesn't mean you need to live in shame because you don't know how all of this is going to work out.

Your story isn't the same as anyone else's. You will need to go through similar steps as I did to get free, but the length of time and intensity of each step will vary from person to person. If others seem to get freedom before you, celebrate them! Celebrate their victory and the hope they can give you. If they can get freedom, so can you.

Tools in the Master's Hands

If the weight of the process seems overwhelming, take a deep breath. You don't have to tackle it all at one time. Healing won't come all at once. If you've been around counselors for any length of time, you might have heard the expression, "Humans are like onions; God peels away the pain one layer at a time." No truer statement has ever been spoken.

We tend to get excited over instant miracles in the Bible. Yet, we often forget that the people in the Bible, much like us, had a period of waiting before they came into full healing. Many miracles happened in an instant, but there are often small miracles that happened in the person's heart long before the moment of full deliverance. Maybe you've gone to counseling but nothing seems to have changed yet. Maybe you tried to believe what God says about you, but you still hate yourself. I get it. It takes time to unwind decades of negative thinking.

Before all this happened, I had goals and dreams for my life. A year in, I thought surely this season would be over soon and I would be able to move towards my future goals with that minor speed bump behind me. But somehow, I found myself in a pit that only seemed to get deeper with time. It was embarrassing at the least and felt hopeless at worst. God should be able to heal me, I assumed.

But why hasn't He? Why am I going through year after year with all these promises of hope in the Bible, only to experience the reality of none of them? Why do I see people get prayed for and receive immediate healing? Is God mad at me?

I wanted nothing more than to be free. Yet, it seemed like I would perpetually live on God's operating table with His scalpel digging and prodding into my heart. The Bible says we should expect suffering if we want to be raised to glory in Christ (Rom 8:17). I wondered if that meant this was my lot in life. Was the only hope for experiencing freedom on the other side of heaven?

So many of those conflicting and confusing thoughts raced through my mind as I went through this process. I couldn't seem to function like other normal people. I wasn't happy like them or energetic like them. My mind was too scattered to dream. It seemed all my dreams died the day I had the mental break. It made no sense why Jesus would die for me, only to let me pay the penalty for my sin through a long, painful life. While I often questioned if He was the one twisting my heart into a million pieces, after several years, I saw **He was actually healing me**.

The pain that I experienced through the process of healing, over time, stopped defaming God's character and showed me the depths of His heart. He isn't a monster or an overbearing dictator. He is gentle, loving and kind. So, He slowly peels away the layers, little by little, day by day. It will feel agonizing most days. You will want to scream when your heart feels like it's cracked wide open, bleeding out on the floor. It may seem like the pain will kill you.

It may seem like **God** is trying to kill you. He isn't.

The slow, agonizing steps of counseling and prayer are tools in the Master's hands. The book of Hebrews says the Word will slice you open and cut you to the core. It will reveal your deepest sins and darkest secrets (Heb 4:12). When you choose to open yourself up to God, prepare for the stinking rot of your past to seep out in the most uncomfortable ways. Yet, while the stench permeates and the pain festers, know the tools the Master handles are for your healing.

Don't get me wrong, He will cut you, but He will be gentle. The reason it takes so long to heal is because God doesn't rush. He wants you to survive the process. While we scream and scrawl for the pain to stop, He is masterfully and slowly removing the chains that bind us. He is slow, because we could not handle having all of our pain removed at once. It would be too much; having thirty-plus years of pain unravel in a day would have destroyed me.

While it may seem less painful than to keep on the way you've been going, if you're reading this book, I have a funny feeling it's because you realized you can't keep going that way anymore. You may have had a mental breakdown like I did, or overdosed, or something worse. I imagine it's because you've come to the end of yourself. You've been in pain a long time. You've been searching for answers and coping the best you could, yet it only got worse. You got deeper into depression, anxiety, paranoia or shame.

The more we rely on ourselves, the further our pits go. While God doesn't put you in a pit, **He won't force you to stop digging one either.** He'll tap on the door of your heart over and over. You'll hear that little whisper telling you to read the Bible, or tell a friend about your dark thoughts or to go to counseling. You'll feel that tug to put the bottle down or flush the pills. But God isn't going to show up in your bathroom and flush them for you.

After a while, if you keep ignoring Him, He will step out of the way and let you dig your pit. He will let you hit rock bottom. He will let you go as far as you can into darkness until you realize you can't find the light without Him. God will let you dig that pit, but rest assured friend, the second you call on Him, He will hop in the pit with you and show you the way out.

If you feel frustration that Jesus let things get this bad for you, surrender that right now. Set that bitterness down and forgive the Lord for His perceived slight. He wasn't slighting you. He was honoring you by letting you go as far as you did. Jesus won't force you to listen to Him. He is patient and kind. Unfortunately, our stubbornness creates calluses over our ears and we tune out the gentle voice of our Father. So, we end up not taking a hold of the kindness Jesus offers and get what "we wanted" instead.

Thankfully, Jesus never runs out of kindness. He is always waiting for us to turn back. So, if you are ready to let God off the hook for letting you self-destruct, so you could see with your own eyes that you need Him, then that will be the moment the walls of your house begin to appear. The foundation is built on trusting God's heart and taking thoughts captive, but the walls of security and peace are built when you begin to lean into Him and trust His timing and process.

It's so important to lean into Him like we talked about in the last chapter when we dissected Isaiah 26:3. Renewing your mind takes work. Surrendering your pain is hard. Many things you will do in recovery will take a lot of effort on your part and it will often seem like your entire life revolves around healing. It will feel like you wake up with a sword in your hand, fighting an invisible enemy every second of the day, while you are also doing all the other everyday things you have to do.

Holding down a job, going through school, maintaining a home and a family are all big responsibilities. When you add fighting for healing on top of that, it can easily get overwhelming. So give yourself space to cry, rest and take big, deep breaths as often as needed. Lean into God's unlimited resources and let Him replenish you when the fight wears you down. The enemy wants nothing more than for us to look at our symptoms, the length of time it takes for us to heal and give up hope on ourselves and God. You may hear thoughts like:

You won't get through this.

You are stuck like this forever.

Stop trying. This is your lot in life.

Every one of those ideas are lies (Phil 1:6, Rom 15:13, Jer 17:14, John 15:11, John 14:27, 2 Thess 3:16). Though, as I've already said, recovery is long and grueling. Most days it looks like two steps forward and ten steps back. So, it's easy for the enemy to come into those moments of weakness and speak despair and resignation over you. In the natural world, healing doesn't make sense. What we've been taught about healing in the mainstream media and what it actually entails are so different.

Our culture says, "See a therapist a few times, shake it off and move on." Yet, if you talk to any of the counselors at the Anxiety Centre or holistic doctors who pursue natural forms of healing, they will tell you that real healing is painful and takes time. We expect that "getting the junk out," mentally or physically, will look like a slow downhill progression into a wide river valley of peace. We expect little by little, day by day, it just gets easier and easier; but that is not how it works. You will not heal at exactly a 15% rate each day you do the right work.

The days you are walking in suffocating darkness without a light in sight are scary and draining. Though, when you have several good days, followed by a random symptom spike, is disheartening to say the least. But that's what this chapter is all about. This chapter is here to teach you that on those days when you are in unrelenting pain, God is there and He is working. A few good days, followed by a few bad ones, doesn't mean God has left you or healing isn't possible.

If I am being honest, I hate how loud pain is when it leaves. It would be great if we could address our traumas without nightmares, panic attacks, etc manifesting as they come to the surface. It would be great if I didn't have to acknowledge and feel every painful memory for it to be addressed. But, that's how it works.

Much like surgery, healing is painful and the process it takes to heal can be as painful as the trauma itself. You have to feel it to heal it. You have to name it, to get rid of it. If we don't face our greatest fears and deepest wounds, we can't move beyond them. I think that is why the enemy works so hard to keep us isolated and ashamed of our pain.

I used to view sadness as a weakness. Crying in public was a cardinal sin in my eyes. I did everything I could to bottle up my feelings and not let anyone know how "weak" I perceived myself to be. When the Lord began to break me of this, He showed me that processing emotion is the only way through it. If you bottle it, you will relive it over and over again. Though it's painful, naming and processing it is the best and fastest way to rid yourself of it.

Which is why the enemy spent most of my life tricking me into believing sadness was a weakness that I had no business sharing with others. If I suppressed it, I could never figure out where the pain stemmed from. If I never named the pain, I wouldn't process it. If I didn't process it, I would live out of a place of hurt forever. Then, the enemy could easily convince me that suffering is all there is in life.

Even though healing is hard and takes time, it is worth the fight. Your growth is worth the fight. Your future is worth the fight. YOU are worth the fight. No one gets better by bottling pain or refusing to change toxic patterns of thinking. We have to lean into God's guidance and grace as we walk the journey towards freedom. Only He truly knows what is in our hearts and the best path forward for us to heal. Let's stop here and take a moment to reflect. Review these questions with the Father, then finish reading the last section.

- Have you avoided receiving healing up to this point? If so, why?

- If you've begun your healing journey, have you doubted God's been in it with you? Why or why not?

- What things in this chapter have helped you doubt His process less?

- What scriptures/takeaways can you apply as a part of your every day routine to lean into the process more?

Trusting God and the process is essential to building a strong house of healing. I tried many times to take over the process and drove myself crazy searching for a magical cure that would end the pain faster than it seemed God would allow. But the problem is that God knows us better than we know ourselves. He knows every single layer of your onion and/or heart.

He knows why you put on a strong face, but cry yourself to sleep at night.

He knows why you make plans with friends but always cancel at the last minute.

He knows why you can't trust people of the opposite sex.

God knows every single ache, pain and misbelief you have. So, if I can give you a piece of advice about the process, it's this: **don't try to figure it out.** Don't try to fix yourself. Don't force yourself into every cleanse, bible study and/or therapy session that your brain can hold. Let Him guide you.

Let Him show you what layer to address and when. If the bitterness you currently struggle with keeps coming to mind, take it as a sign that He wants to work on that and work on it. You don't need to keep a running list of all your issues and obsessively pray over your faults. God is gentle and patient. He will show you what to handle and what order to handle it in based on how painful events and toxic habits are interwoven.

My counselor once told me that "Anger is the bodyguard for sadness." Hearing that blew me away because of the implications it has for healing. You could be up to your eyeballs in anger and bitterness. You may not remember the last day you woke up without feeling irritated. Yet, you feel God keep talking to you about trauma and sorrow. It may not make sense. You may wonder why God isn't addressing "the issue" and if you would be better off handling it on your own.

You aren't. I promise. I tried many, many times and had to come crawling back to God after thinking I knew better and made it harder on myself because I didn't let Him lead. God knows if your anger is an anger issue or if your anger is a self protection mechanism for sadness. You may not have the insight to figure that out. So, let Him lead. Trust His guiding hand (Is 58:11).

The process of healing is hard. There is no doubt about that. But we make it harder on ourselves when we try to lead and refuse to let God be God. If you want to run from Him and dig a pit, He will let you dig a pit. If you think you know better and want to fix yourself, He will let you fix yourself. Though, the best and most effective way to healing is walking behind Him.

Let Him clear and carve the path before you. Let Him gently walk you by the hand through the valley of the shadow of death. There is life on the other side. We serve a God who raises people from the dead. He knows exactly how to bring you back to life.

Chapter 5:
SEEING CLEARLY IN THE DARK

In the months before my mental breakdown, life was as good as it had been in a long time. I was actually really happy. I can remember one day in particular, when I was jumping around at my condo with all sorts of energy, doing cartwheels and handstands while talking to my roommate. I told her how grateful I was for my health and my life. The year before, I nearly had a nervous breakdown from the stress of dental bills, a friend overdosing, my aunt passing away from cancer and the ending of an unhealthy relationship.

2016 was not my year, but 2017 looked like it might be.

I started a new job, a new Bible study and was making new friends. My health seemed to be better than ever. Shortly before my meltdown, I saw a glimpse of what living in peace could be like. So, I stood upside down in my room that day, thanking God for how healthy I seemed to be. I was blessed, I had survived the storms of the year before and I believed life was about to get really good.

If only it were that easy; if only all we had to do was survive challenging events in life and not face physical and emotional repercussions afterward. Some people assume that surviving trauma is the only step to handling it. Unfortunately, that isn't the case and that assumption doesn't explain why many people have mental breakdowns "out of the blue." I'm sure you've heard people say things like this before:

"Everything was fine, then wham, I had a massive panic attack. I don't know where it came from."

"Life isn't that bad right now, but I can't shake this depression. I don't even know why I am sad."

"I can't sleep. I don't know why I can't sleep. My mind just won't shut off."

Over and over again, people just like you and me have these "out-of-the-blue" experiences with anxiety and depression that really aren't that random at all. They are the result of that cup we talked about in chapter two being filled to the brim and spilling over. For people struggling with depression, that cup may be mixed with grief and stress because depression isn't a direct result of stress hyperstimulation.

Though, grief doesn't have a formula for how it reveals itself either. It can be just as much of a jerk as our nervous system and have really obnoxious ways of coming to the surface. More often than not, there are "quiet periods" where only minor symptoms appear and everything seems OK. These "lag times" deceive people into thinking the stress overload came on all of a sudden, when really it's been brewing for years and you are only now seeing the results of stress and trauma from the past.

At the beginning of 2017, I was living in one of those "quiet periods." All seemed right with the world; I was happy, healthy and carefree. Then that horrible day came when I found myself curled up in the fetal position on my bed questioning if Jesus was real. *How could this happen?* I had just conquered one of my greatest fears by speaking in front of a room full of strangers. I believed God had brought me out of the worst year of my life and into the "Promised Land." Though it appeared to be "out of the blue," it was anything but.

It was the culmination of decades of unresolved grief.

It was years of allowing others to dictate who I was.

It was every time God tried to draw me close, to heal my aching heart and I pushed Him away, sure that I could handle it myself. In that moment, in the fetal position on my bed, I wasn't just cradling confusion about who Jesus was; **I was cradling the weight of trying to heal myself for the last decade.** The warning signs were there for years: the panic attacks that "seemed manageable," the hallucinations that came and went, my low self-esteem that led me to date boys I knew didn't care about me.

My cup was getting a little more full each day. My body and brain were trying to warn me that things "under the surface" were not good. All of it pointed to a heart that needed healing, but I ignored it. I didn't want to deal with it. I didn't want to have to relive the things that happened that brought me there in the first place.

I think this is a common human response to pain. We want to do anything to make it stop; so we ignore it, numb it and do whatever it takes to make it go away, instead of the hardest thing, which is facing it. There is so much pain in this life, it can be overwhelming at times. It can seem like pain is all there is. Though, I'm hoping that after we've talked about God's heart for healing, you are beginning to hope there is something more.

Since this world does seem to be full of pain and even if we can heal it we all have to endure it to some degree, we have to wonder, *What is the point of it all? Is there a purpose in our pain?* To answer that question, I want to share with you what the Lord shared with me early on in this process that I did not understand until years later. In the summer of 2017, while I was studying the Bible, I read Isaiah 6 and this is what verses 1-8 say:

> "In the year that King Uzziah died, I saw the Lord, high and exalted, seated on a throne; and the train of his robe filled the temple. Above him were seraphim, each with six wings: With two wings they covered their faces, with two they covered their feet, and with two they were flying. And they were calling to one another:
>
> 'Holy, holy, holy is the Lord Almighty; the whole earth is full of his glory.'
>
> At the sound of their voices the doorposts and thresholds shook and the temple was filled with smoke.

'Woe to me!' I cried. 'I am ruined! For I am a man of unclean lips, and I live among a people of unclean lips, and my eyes have seen the King, the Lord Almighty.'

Then one of the seraphim flew to me with a live coal in his hand, which he had taken with tongs from the altar. With it, he touched my mouth and said, 'See, this has touched your lips; your guilt is taken away and your sin atoned for.'

Then I heard the voice of the Lord saying, 'Whom shall I send? And who will go for us?'

And I said, 'Here am I. Send me!'"

As I read those verses, they leaped off the page and into my heart. I knew God was speaking to me. This is what people mean when they say "the Lord highlighted a verse to me." God's Word can have literal and abstract applications. He wrote every word in the Bible with a specific intent, but because God's ways are higher than our ways, He is able to take the exact same words He spoke to a prophet in Israel thousands of years ago and use them to speak to a girl in Tennessee in 2017.

Shortly after reading that verse, I ended up in 1 Corinthians 10 and God highlighted another verse to me. 1 Corinthians 10:13 says this:

> "No temptation has overtaken you except what is common to mankind. And God is faithful; he will not let you be tempted beyond what you can bear. But when you are tempted, he will also provide a way out so that you can endure it."

These two verses, put together, paint a very clear picture of a person going through a trial with the intent of purifying and cleansing them so they can fulfill the call God has placed on their life. Neither of these verses say God plotted with the devil to take me out. They don't say He enjoys seeing His kids in pain if it makes them more holy.

SEEING CLEARLY IN THE DARK

Lamentations 3:32-33 is clear that God doesn't enjoy bringing suffering on mankind. Though, He will allow us to be tested so that the purity of our hearts can be revealed and refined if we allow it (See the book of Job). While the Lord "highlighted" those verses to me specifically, I think there are a few applications that we can all pull from them.

A. Even though it feels unfair that you are in a pit so dark you can't imagine seeing light again, God has a plan for you. He didn't let you get that far without having a path for your escape planned.

B. This pit is a part of your testimony and your calling. Had I not gone through these last six years, I wouldn't be writing this book today. When God saw me, screaming in pain, begging for an easy out month after month, He said no. He had my freedom in mind, but He also had yours in mind too. Had He given me an easy escape route, and He certainly could have, I never would've learned the things I am sharing with you today.

C. If God gave me an easy-out a second before He knew I was ready, I would've landed myself right back there not too long after. I had to get these lessons rooted down deep in my soul. I not only had to believe they were true, but I had to learn to walk them out long before I could begin to teach them. God let me get to my breaking point. God let me be tried and tested in ways I couldn't fathom were possible. God gave me what I needed not only to get free, but to stay free.

Let those verses be hope for you. Let them remind you that trials will come; pain will come. God didn't shield Himself from pain when He walked on this earth in human form. Jesus endured every ache and pain you and I will ever go through. So, we can't expect Him to shield us from everything life throws at us.

There is beauty in Him being our defender, our hiding place and our safe refuge (Ps 91). But there is also beauty in realizing He is the strength and power that enables us to stand and fight against the evils in the world . . . and in our minds. Realizing that God never allowed me to go through this to harm me, and that

House of Healing

He always had my healing in mind, has been one of the most important things I've learned along the way. I pray through this book you will inch your way closer and closer to seeing God as your healer, even when it feels like He couldn't be further from that.

After I received that word from God and He showed me a bird's eye view of what the next six years would look like, things only got worse. The temptation came harder. The warfare got stronger. The day came when I heard that demon whisper evil things to me and my thoughts took on a whole new level of darkness.

God sharing that prophetic insight through His Word didn't make going through it any easier. I didn't understand what it meant until years later. Oppression can blind you from the truth that's sitting right in front you. Fear makes you irrational, creating a tornado of chaos that whips around every ounce of rationale you have, leaving you confused at best and hopeless at worst.

But this is where we have a choice. In the midst of our own personal nightmares, we get to decide if we trust God will do something **in** our pain and **with** our pain. Because that tornado can either destroy you or it can build you. You can partner with God and allow Him to control each movement of the wind so the sharp edges of your heart aren't battered, but shaped into something beautiful.

I came across an old article by Glynnis Whitwer[5] the other day and want to share the powerful truth it reminded me of. She said, "Don't doubt in the dark, what you know to be true in the light." Friend, even though you may not feel God's hand with you right now, if you have ever seen Him show up in your life, cling to that. He hasn't changed.

His love is everlasting and King David went so far as to say it's better than life itself (Ps 63:3). He never leaves or forsakes us (Heb 13:5). So, do as the psalmists do and call to mind the things God has done for you while you are in this season of refining and recovery. Remind yourself that He can turn darkness into light and chaos into calling.

This is the fight you and I both have to face; trusting God with the "now" and believing there is more waiting in the future. While you're in recovery, you will have to wake up every day and decide who you will believe. Will you choose to pray and trust God is working even when you can't see the results? Will you get mad, blame God and sit in misery?

Can I tell you a secret?

I blamed God . . . a lot. I blamed God for way more than I'd like to admit. So, please do us both a favor and don't fight Him. Don't point a finger at God as if His motives for letting you endure this are anything but pure. The Bible promises us that suffering produces good things.

Romans 5:3-5 says:

> "Not only so, but we also glory in our sufferings, because we know that suffering produces perseverance; perseverance, character; and character, hope. And hope does not put us to shame, because God's love has been poured out into our hearts through the Holy Spirit, who has been given to us."

James 1:2-4 says:

> "Consider it pure joy, my brothers and sisters, whenever you face trials of many kinds, because you know that the testing of your faith produces perseverance. Let perseverance finish its work so that you may be mature and complete, not lacking anything."

Right here, in His Word, God promises that the suffering we endure can produce amazing results: the maturity, growth, hope and joy we all want. Who would've guessed it? Right smack dab in the middle of scriptures on suffering is a recipe for growth and joy. If mind renewal and trusting God are the foundation for our house of healing, and trusting God's process creates the walls, then finding purpose and joy is the window through which we want to frame our perspective.

We can experience joy when we choose to count our blessings. The blessings may not be obvious. These scriptures show us we have to frame every painful experience through the windows of joy because we know what suffering can produce. **Every time we experience pain, it's an opportunity for growth and healing.** God wants our healing more than we do, but He sees our future through the lens of a much larger picture. Sometimes we have to face the hard things to reveal the healing that needs to be done. Our immediate comfort isn't always what produces the best long term results.

So, let it burn.

Let it hurt.

Don't run from it.

Don't dull it.

Face it.

Feel it.

Conquer it.

Thank God for every single moment of it because each moment you struggle, you are growing. You are healing. That's why James says we can rejoice in our suffering. While we don't rejoice over abuse or negative thinking patterns that bring pain, we can rejoice for what God will do in spite of it.

Think of Joseph from the book of Genesis. That man suffered. Truly, he was right alongside Job in the things he endured on earth. He was a slave in Egypt for decades. Even though he had favor with God in Egypt, he had to endure abuse as a slave. He was ripped away from his family as a teenager, sold into slavery by his own flesh and blood. None of it was fair. Talk about not "living your best life."

SEEING CLEARLY IN THE DARK

Yet, we don't hear of him blaming God for it one time. We don't hear him complaining about his situation at all. It's hard for me to believe a teenage boy never whined about such a sucky situation. Though we don't see it in Scripture, so at the very least, we know complaint and bitterness didn't define his story.

After living in slavery for years, he was thrown into jail for being accused of raping Potiphar's wife. If abuse, neglect and being sold by your own family weren't enough, it seems like a good dose of wrongful accusation would make things just perfect. You have to know the devil tempted him with thoughts like, *God doesn't love you. If He did, He would've let you out of slavery years ago.*

You ended up in jail after being made a slave. Give up, you're worthless to God!

Sure, you earned some favor with your master, but God doesn't care about you enough to rescue you.

You know the enemy had to heap mountains of shame onto him when he interpreted dreams for the baker and butler, then was left in jail for years after the fact. Joseph could've compared himself to everyone around him. He could've become bitter for being allowed to suffer harder and longer than most people. No one else in his family ended up in slavery. Why did he have to?

I think the reason Joseph "thrived" in slavery, to the point that people noticed him, was because he resisted all thought processes that began with self-pity and ended with comparison. He let bitterness have no place in his heart. He let God use him right where he was. He let his story unfold exactly as God allowed it to. He let the pain drive him to the Lord instead of away from Him.

At the exact moment God intended, Joseph saw what all the pain was about. In the blink of an eye, God took him from the prison to the palace. He became the second in command to Pharaoh and was a critical part of saving his family, the Israelites and the Egyptians from a famine. Joseph took on a huge place of influence in a matter of minutes. Then, after all that waiting, he finally saw what God had been up to.

God knew there would be a famine.

God knew he would need someone on the inside to protect people from starving.

God knew He would give Pharoah a dream and have Joseph in the exact spot He needed to interpret it.

God worked in the midst of the evil the enemy had planned for Joseph, all the while creating a masterful plan of redemption for him and his country. Not to mention, Joseph's character was refined by the time he got the leading role in Pharaoh's court. All that time he spent suffering, God was refining his character to handle his calling. It wasn't all for nothing; God truly loved him and wanted to use him in a mighty way. Joseph just had to trust God.

The same goes for you and me. We can't compare our stories to anyone else. We can't believe that when we suffer harder or longer than those around us, God has somehow forgotten about us or doesn't love us. I can remember so many times when I'd get jealous of people who seemed to "never suffer anything" and it appeared I was always going through something.

That jealousy created a huge root of bitterness, which isolated me beyond what my own pain did. The enemy will stop at nothing to steal your joy. The last thing he wants is for you to see your pain as purposeful, use it to fulfill your destiny and have peace and hope during your road to recovery.

What destruction comes to the kingdom of darkness when we look at our suffering through the "windows" of joy because we trust that God brings all things together for good (Rom 8:28). At that point, we are untouchable. We enjoy the life we are living in the moment, no matter how painful. Then, when the refining season is over, we walk in more freedom and joy than ever before. Satan can't do anything to a person like that. That kind of ruthless trust is impenetrable.

Chapter 6:
SHUT THE DOOR!

If you grew up in the South, you'll likely have fond memories of summertime. Swimming, barbecues, late sunsets and cricket serenades are only a few of the charms of summer in the Delta. While there are many things to love about that time of year, there's one thing that no summer sunset can make better. That my friend is bugs, mosquitoes to be exact.

Come Memorial Day, every river, pond, front porch, back porch and square inch of swarmable property will be covered with those nasty little pests. You can't get away from them. You can spend an entire cookout swattin' them away too. After being bit fifty times, sometimes it's easier to give up and let them have their way with you until they get blood drunk and move on.

Though memories of swattin' bugs are never too far gone before another season rolls around, there's another memory that I, and any child raised in the South, won't soon forget. It's the moment you're standing with the front door wide open, talking to a friend. Maybe your crush stopped by to say, "Hello." Just when you lean and stretch the door further open, smiling, with butterflies jumpin' around in your stomach, from the depths of your mother's bowels comes a yell so guttural you'd think she just found out you murdered someone.

But that's not it.

Somehow, from the kitchen that has no view of the front door, she has eyed your front door holdin' self and screams, "Shut the door! You're letting in all the bugs!" Yes, all those Count Dracula-esque critters snuck their way past your distracted gaze and into your home. Naturally, your mom isn't happy, as any parent would be when you let all the bugs in and cool air out.

Because every good Southern momma knows what we all do; doors are made to keep the good things in and the bad things out. We have to keep guard over our doors. When we get distracted by

House of Healing

something pleasing to the eye, we can easily miss things sneaking into our safe space and end up with an infestation faster than we can blink. So it is with our hearts. Proverbs 4:23 tells us, "Above all else, guard your heart, for everything you do flows from it."

Everything you do flows from it.

Our hearts and/or thoughts are the only access point the enemy has to us. Satan can not come in and take over our lives unless we allow him to. We allow him to do this by watching, listening to and/or doing things that don't line up with God's Word. Just like the home you live in now, it is your job to monitor what comes in and out of your thought life the same way you would the front door. If demonic influences and/or negative thinking are let in, may I say that those little critters will ruin the nice home ya' just started buildin'.

Early on in my recovery, I threw myself into demonic freedom sessions, hoping and praying they would rid me of the anxiety. Demonic freedom sessions are prayer meetings where people gather around someone with the intent of praying a demon away from them. There is a lot of debate on the subject because of how people have approached this practice and doubt that Christians can be oppressed by demons.

I assumed I had a demon attached to me since I heard Lord Voldemort speak to me that day. *Surely a few prayer sessions would be able to rid me of this nightmare,* I thought. Yet, it wasn't that simple. I think the hardest part about understanding the supernatural is we are dealing with a realm we can't see. So, we have to look for signs of evil influence in people's behavior the same way we would look for positive changes in a person's life as evidence of having fruit of the Holy Spirit

Hollywood has done a great job desensitizing people to the reality of the demonic through movies that make demons appear no more real than the Easter Bunny. This process has apparently reached its climax now that our culture worships satan openly and as a whole Americans think nothing about it. He's just another

SHUT THE DOOR!

"god" among the many honored in this pagan country. These days, we "love who we love" and worship whoever we want to worship, even if it is the prince of darkness.

Yet, people are broken, hurting and more mentally tormented than ever. We are blind to the obvious, spiritual root while mocking those who would dare to believe in anything that can't be dissected in a science lab. Could Hollywood have gotten it wrong? Is it possible that when people appear possessed, they actually are? Now, more than ever, we need truth. We need to face the facts that the "fruit" of our culture turning away from God is mental unwellness and a nation ransacked by demonic influence. Even if it seems outdated to believe spirits can torment people, it might be time to revisit the ways of old, because what we are currently doing is not working.

While I fully believe demons are real and deliverance ministry is necessary, I also know people who have been scarred by the mishandling of demonic freedom sessions. I assume some of you may have seen or heard some scary things done to others in the name of Jesus. These experiences may have led you to believe all those people were crazy, or worse, what they were doing was unbiblical. While I know there probably have been situations that weren't handled in the gentlest manner, it doesn't negate the reality of demonic influence and the need for demonic deliverance.

Now that we understand demons can interfere in our lives, we have to ask the question, "How much influence can they actually have?"

If you follow Christ, a demon can not possess you. When you give yourself over to the Lord, His Spirit **possesses** you (Eph 1:13-14). However, we can give space in our lives to demonic **oppression** if we turn from God and engage in sinful/demonic activity i.e. leave our doors open. I can not tell you what it is like to be possessed. But I can tell you I have been heavily oppressed by demonic influence and that was quite enough for me to say I don't want anything to do with it.

When God says to have nothing to do with the occult, pornography, drugs, etc, He says that for our benefit, not His (Deut 18:9-12, 1 Cor 6:18, Zeph 1:4-6). If He says "shut the door" to things that don't "seem" like they are that bad, trust Him and just do it. If a TV show or song feels off to you, don't listen to it. If there's a person around you who is playing with tarot cards or crystals, you need to leave.

I didn't end up in the pit because I opened myself up to witchcraft or the occult. While some might say "sowing your wild oats" for a decade or so, like I did, is just a part of growing up, there's really no sin that's OK for us to let slide. If you wouldn't leave your front door partially cracked so a few mosquitoes can get in, why would you leave any doors to your heart open to evil influences? It doesn't matter which door satan enters. If you give him an inch, he will take a mile. If you let him in, he isn't going to leave without a fight.

There are stories all through the New Testament of people oppressed by demons (Lk 13:11, Mark 9:25, Matt 8:14-17). It is very possible that some of you reading this have a spirit of depression, fear, or suicide tormenting you. However, I found, like some people, that my problems were more complex than a few prayer sessions could fix. The good news is that if your mental health issues are only rooted in demonic oppression, it is somewhat easier and much faster to remove a demon than it is to do the painful work of counseling and renewing the mind. It is possible that a door to the demonic was opened through something you or someone in your family did, and there is nothing else keeping you bound.

Though, in my experience, some people don't get immediately set free from deliverance sessions because they have work in their hearts and minds they need to do to keep the demonic influences out for good (Luke 11:24-26). For example, if you hate yourself and regularly say out loud that you are a disgusting, worthless person, you will attract demonic spirits through that sin. Even if someone is able to set you free from demonic oppression through prayer, you essentially keep your front door wide open and welcome demonic influences back into your house by agreeing with the lie that you have no value.

Dealing with the spiritual is an important step in learning to walk in freedom. But because humans are complex creatures and the spiritual is tied into the mental, which is tied into the physical, it's not always as simple as praying for demons to flee and seeing them stay gone, without any other work being done. Though, you need to know about this step. So many American churches do themselves an injustice by denying demons existence and influence in their lives. If we keep in line with what Scripture says, there's no way we can deny that the spirit world is real and has a real impact on the way we live (Eph 6, James 4:7, 1 John 4:4, 1 Pet 5:8-9, 2 Thess 3:3).

But you don't have to live in fear of demons lurking behind every door, waiting on your next mistake so they can take over your life. What Jesus did on the Cross fully stripped satan of his authority over us (Col 2:15). He has no right to our lives anymore, unless we give him access through our sin (Eph 4:26). I know it may seem harsh, but some of you may be where you are mentally because there is a sin you haven't let go of yet. Trust me, the last thing I wanted to hear was that my recovery wasn't anyone else's responsibility but my own.

While you may have been abused for years and come to believe awful things about yourself because of that treatment, if you continue to agree with those lies, you are essentially giving the devil free reign over your mind. That is the epitome of sin. I say this so directly because I would be doing you a disservice by sugar-coating the truth and not getting directly to the root of the matter. **You can not agree with the devil and live in peace.** It will never happen.

Living in shame, fear and anger may feel good because it's comfortable. It may be all you know. Though, like I've said so many times already, the foundation in your house of healing is trusting God's word and taking control over what you can take control over - your mind. You may have had the front door to your house wide open for years. You may just now be realizing that you have control over who or what you let in.

If that's you, don't beat yourself up for being unaware. Just commit to living differently in the future. Commit to asking Jesus for help anytime you accidentally open the door to wrong things and be ready to get rid of anything He says isn't good for you. We can not fight off the demonic on our own. Being surrendered to God and letting Him fight for/with us is key to getting and staying free.

I battled being fully surrendered for a long time. I can remember telling my counselor about halfway through my recovery period, "I think a part of me is holding back from Jesus. I am scared to give Him everything. So, this fear I have toward my thoughts is my way of defending myself. I have a hard time trusting Jesus can protect me. So, I feel like I have to be on guard all day long. Even though I am protecting myself in the wrong way, a part of it comes from not trusting God."

We will do some of the most bizarre things to protect ourselves from pain, right? Like putting ourselves in more misery because we assume full surrender to an invisible God is scarier. While I explained all of this to my counselor, I used the analogy of having one room of my heart still locked. I had opened the door to Him and let Him go room by room through my house, but something in me was terrified of giving Him my all.

What if I really am crazy for believing in an invisible God?

What if I give my heart to Him and nothing gets better?

What if He doesn't love me as much as I hope He does?

All of those same, heart wrenching doubts swirled through my mind as I debated giving my heart over to the God I was beginning to love. It took me a long time to go from seeing God as angry and callous, like I did as a teen, to being ready to open the last lock on the deepest places of my heart. It is still a day-by-day process. There are days where I unintentionally push Jesus to the side and swing the front door of my heart wide open so negative thoughts and influences can come in.

Some days it's easy, it seems like nothing tempts me to watch things I shouldn't watch or do things I shouldn't do. But then there are days where I am tired or emotional, so I turn on a trashy TV show or something else I know I don't need to watch. I can justify it a million different ways; the silliest one is, "I want to watch something easy. I just don't want to think right now."
If I continue down that path for long, I can start to find myself falling prey to comparison, discontentment and other negative thinking patterns. While I am not saying that demons will oppress you every time you watch the Kardashians, I am saying at the very least the things we put into our minds/hearts should **draw us closer to Christ** and not **away from Him.**

Those little compromises add up over time. What you may see as just "entertainment" now, could lead to a sin that opens a door for the demonic to enter later. We have to guard our eyes and ears because they are the entry ways to our heart. Proverbs 4 says this:

> "My son, pay attention to what I say; turn your ear to my words.
> Do not let them out of your sight, keep them within your heart;
> for they are life to those who find them and health to one's whole body." (Prov 4:20-22)

In reference to this scripture Joseph Prince says:

> "God tells us to guard what we hear, what we see, and what is in our hearts. He wants us to have our ears full of the gracious words of Jesus, our eyes full of the presence of Jesus and our hearts meditating on what we have heard and seen in Jesus . . . It is all about beholding Jesus, and as we behold Him, we are transformed more and more into His likeness, full of unmerited favor and truth!

"Don't miss this powerful promise, my friend. The result of tuning our ear- and eye-gates to Jesus is that He will be life and health to us . . . If we are only feeding on the news media, magazines, or the unending stream of information on the Internet, it is no wonder that we feel weak and tired. There is just no nourishment for us there . . . Be wise—don't overdose yourself on information and knowledge that does not infuse you with God's life and power."[6]

God's word is life to us. If we feed on it, we will have no choice but to prosper because of it. The same goes for letting evil things into our eyes and ears. If you feed on evil, you will grow in evil. As we have seen with American culture, many people are lured into evil because they are deceived into ignoring the influence of the demonic realm. They say watching violent or sexually graphic shows don't affect their hearts and minds. Similarly, people worship the devil without any thought as to why that might end up bad for them.

If you are a non-believer, the weight of the spiritual significance of your choices doesn't change, though I understand why you may believe it does. Though, for the Christian, we have warning after warning in the Bible on paying attention to what we watch and listen to. So, there is no excuse for opening ourselves up to toxic messaging. While I believe everything we do **can** have a spiritual implication, there are many things that only have negative or positive implications based on the person using it.

For example, social media in and of itself is not good or evil. It does not have a will or a spirit, so it can't choose to do good or evil. But people can manipulate the programs and use them for anything they want to; so can the spirit realm. In that sense, some things are neutral and not inherently evil. On the other hand, content that is violent or obviously rooted in the occult is not OK to consume because you believe only weak people are affected by it.

Violence is violence no matter how you spin it. Occult activity is the same. It doesn't matter how strong you perceive yourself to

SHUT THE DOOR!

be. In reality, you should want your spirit to be sensitive to evil things so you don't inundate yourself with them and become desensitized. We are in a war between light and dark, good and evil. The things we consume either make us more like the Father of Lights or . . . the prince of darkness.

That doesn't mean you are only allowed to watch things that discuss Jesus if you want to live a peace filled life. But it does mean if you choose to watch a comedian, what that comedian says shouldn't violate God's laws of love. He/she can tell all kinds of jokes about family, work and life. But if you keep watching while they make explicit references, then you are just as bad as a googly eyed kid, standing at the door letting in all the mosquitoes.

What will happen if you do it one time? Well, if you are a believer, the Holy Spirit will likely convict you. That will be your opportunity to keep the door to your house shut by listening to His spirit. When He shows you a behavior that could lead to opening your house to evil, simply repent, stop doing it and put it behind you. However, if you continue listening to graphic content, the Lord will pursue you. Though, if you ignore Him, there will come a point where He stops. Like I said in chapter four, the Lord will let you run from Him. He will let you go as far as you want into your pain, your sorrow **or** your sin. His kindness draws us to repentance, but it is also His kindness and love that lets us choose our own way (1 Cor 13).

Some of you reading this may be in the mental state you are in due to behaviors God told you to stop engaging in a long time ago. You may have trauma to deal with. You may also have people to forgive. But part of the reason you may have ended up here is opening yourself up to things you have no business being involved with. I see so many people playing around with tarot cards, crystals and New Age items these days. These things are not new. God is not surprised by your being tempted to gain supernatural wisdom through avenues other than Him.

But you have to realize, if you aren't getting supernatural insight from God, then you are getting it from the devil. There are **no**

neutral spiritual beings. Spirits can think and choose (Luke 11:24-26). So they are light or dark, good or evil, with God or against Him. People who believe they follow impartial "spirit guides," or dead relatives, are following demons. The spirits of our dead relatives do not float around, disembodied on earth, waiting for our help to guide them to eternal paradise.

Once we die, the only option is heaven or hell (2 Cor 5:6). But satan is a deceiver and a liar (John 8:44). He also disguises himself as an angel of light (2 Cor 11:14). He will do whatever it takes to get you to follow him; even if it means taking advantage of your grief by tricking you into interacting with his minions.

If you are engaging in occult practices of any kind, please read Deuteronomy 18:9-12 and Acts 16:16-19 to understand why those things can have no place in your life if you want to live free. As tough as it may be to rid yourself of these things, don't resist conviction if you feel it. That means God hasn't stopped pursuing the issue. This moment is your chance to turn from that and open your heart back up to the Father. We need God every second of the day, especially as we are healing. Don't let things like this get in the way of the beautiful relationship He wants to have with you.

Remember, God warns us about opening our doors to the wrong influences for our benefit, not His. These things not only get in the way of our relationship with Him, they also drag us to places we do not want to go. Christian teacher Jenny Weaver is the perfect example of this. She says that watching one movie about witchcraft changed the entire course of her life. At the point she was turned on to witchcraft, she hated her life and was desperate for control.

One day, she and her friends watched a movie based on a group of girls who lived as witches. What started as a few friends watching a "silly movie," turned into teenage girls taking blood oaths and using witchcraft to manipulate people. The desire she felt to find stability in her life was met through the practice of witchcraft. Instead of turning to God, she got so wrapped up in witchcraft she became a full blown Wiccan. Because she opened herself up to lots of spiritual influences, she also used drugs to open her mind to more of the spirit realm.

The drug use got to a point where it made her feel like she was losing her mind. She ended up homeless and only by the grace of God was saved, delivered and set free. Now, she teaches the Bible and educates people on the dangers of allowing satan in your life through New Age practices, drugs and entertainment. Jenny's story isn't unusual. If you allow the demonic into your life, it will slowly but surely take over. We have to surrender to God's word and follow His lead if we want to live in peace.

As you've briefly heard Jenny's story and all the other things I've shared in this chapter about guarding your mind/heart, now it's time to take what you've learned and apply it. Go back over the list of toxic behaviors, people you need to forgive, etc., from the prayers in the previous chapters. Also, take some time to consider the movies, podcasts, music and other entertainment you are listening to.

Ask the Lord to highlight what you need to work on first. Let Him show you what doors are the most important to address. There is no way to address every issue at once, so take your time. Even though you may want to hurry up and get all the work done so you can get past the pain, just sit with Jesus in the suck for now, OK? Let Him take you layer by layer, day by day through each pain point or sin issue. He knows you intimately and will walk with you as slowly as needed to make sure everything is healed.

If God shows you that your first step is forgiving your family for abusing you; find a Scripture on forgiveness, write it out and insert the person's name who hurt you. Every time a thought of how they abused you resurfaces and you start to feel angry about it, quote the Scripture out loud and say, "I choose to forgive them." Ask for God's help if your heart isn't in it. It goes against human nature to forgive. We need God to help us walk in His laws of love and freedom.

It will take time, so don't expect the emotions to go away in a few days. It may take weeks, but if you are consistent with letting God walk you through each pain point, He will change your heart. Some situations may take several Scriptures to address. You may need to forgive someone for abuse but at the same time, find a verse on healing a broken heart to address the sadness and pain you feel over that abuse. If God asks you to address only one situation with multiple applications like this, don't get discouraged. Many times, a painful memory has several tough emotions to work through.

Once you have addressed the things God highlights to you, understand that you are engaging in deep spiritual and emotional work. It may seem monotonous and like nothing is happening, but you are breaking ties with the enemy. You are taking your freedom back one step at a time. This work is how you close the door you or someone else opened and learn how to never open it again.

It's also possible that it won't feel monotonous and may feel like you are reverting backwards. Your symptoms may seem to get worse; if they do, don't quit. Once you begin to fight back, the enemy won't let you go easily. You may experience an increase in hard thoughts and feelings. You may have nightmares.

I can't tell you how the enemy will react to this, but I do know he doesn't want you to have freedom. So, he will do whatever he can to convince you the work is pointless and your future is hopeless. Please, whatever you do, don't give up. Those thoughts telling you to quit are a sign that you are onto something. The enemy wouldn't fight you so hard if there wasn't victory on the other side waiting for you. When you're ready, pray this with me:

SHUT THE DOOR!

Father,

Thank You for walking with me through this. Thank You for illuminating the places I need healing and the places I haven't surrendered to You. Show me if there is sin that is keeping me bound. Show me if there are movies, podcasts or relationships that are hindering me from living the life You called me to.

God, I need You to help me let go. Give me strength to release the things that are killing me. Infuse me with Your power when I feel overwhelmed with my bad habits or the influence the enemy has in my life. Thank You for fighting for me and with me.

Amen

Chapter 7:
PRACTICAL TIPS FOR RECOVERY

After trudging through the previous chapter and the weight of the supernatural realm, you may be happy to learn we are going to take a hard right turn away from the demonic. I feel like there might be a few "yay's!" I would hear if I were sitting next to you. While all the talks we've had so far have been great, I wouldn't be doing my job if I didn't also include practical tips you can use in everyday life.

These tips are like common house tools; hammers, screwdrivers, paint and plungers. Anyone **can** use these tools, but many people don't know how or when they need to. But these tools are crucial for maintaining a home and keeping it in good working order. So, let me hand you some basic tools that have served me well and helped me maintain my sanity as I continue my journey for lasting healing and peace.

Yes, I did say continue, because my journey isn't complete yet. As I type this I am working with a doctor to treat some undetermined health issues. In 2021, I experienced some of the most peace filled months of my life. I was happy, healthy and had very limited anxiety symptoms. I thought I had finally reached the point where my house of healing was complete and all I needed to do from there was maintain. However, I forgot the basic tips that I am going to share with you below.

While I don't know whether my excitement to get back to normal life and overuse of caffeine and sugar caused my health issues, what I do know is that I have had to work twice as hard this time around to find lasting healing. After those peace filled months in 2021, I entered a season that felt eerily familiar to what I had just come out of. The symptoms in this "relapse" included insomnia, nausea, racing thoughts, and the list went on.

PRACTICAL TIPS FOR RECOVERY

It was discouraging to say the least. I couldn't believe I found myself in the pit again, especially after all the work I had just done. I don't say this to scare you, but for you to understand if you go through layer after layer of mental/emotional healing and then find that your body needs some TLC, this isn't uncommon. Stress can do crazy things to the body. While I dont know exactly what happened to me, it seems that after four years of chronic stress and anxiety, my body was depleted and began to send me warning signs that my heart wasn't the only thing that needed healing.

So, while you are healing your mind/heart, please take care of your body. Don't think that you can abuse yourself with alcohol, sugar and caffeine during your recovery process and not feel the side effects of it at some point. I pray that you won't go through a "relapse" like me. The better you take care of yourself and follow the tips below, the greater chance you have at seeing lasting recovery come sooner.

So, without further ado, here are ten practical tips for recovery.

1. Ditch the caffeine. Ditch the caffeine. Ditch the caffeine.

I know I am about to crush so many hearts, sorry in advance. If I didn't love you, I wouldn't dare to peel away the ambiguous green label from your warm, over excited fingers. But I think we all need the reminder that caffeine is a stimulant. You can't drink it daily and expect for your body to calm down from stress and/or hyperstimulation. Even if you are struggling with depression, chugging caffeine to get through the day will do horrible things to your body as the caffeine revs it up then causes it to crash. Jim Folk, CEO of Anxiety Centre, said:

> "Since caffeine is a stimulant that stimulates the body, ingesting caffeine into an already anxious and hyperstimulated body is like pouring gas on an already raging fire . . . Kenneth Kendler, director of the Virginia Institute for Psychiatric and Behavioral Genetics, found that

prolonged use of caffeine increased the likelihood of the development of anxiety and depression. The study showed that heavy caffeine users were also almost **twice as likely** to develop panic disorder, generalized anxiety disorder, and major depression."[7]

While you may have thought that caffeine "jitters" were the only negative side effect of consuming caffeine, that couldn't be further from the truth. Our culture is so over-caffeinated. I don't think most of us realize how much caffeine we consume and are naive to its effect on our body. The average small cup of coffee contains around 100mg of caffeine. While the FDA claims an adult can have up to 400mg of caffeine a day safely[8], when you are in recovery, you truly don't need to have any at all.

I know, I know, you're thinking, *How will I survive?* Exercise and vitamins will become your best friends. Getting a good workout first thing in the morning will help wake you up. Taking a shower and ending it with a cold-water rinse is also a nice way to energize your mind and body. You can't overestimate the help of a good multivitamin either. Because the average American diet consists of garbage wrapped in sugar and salt, many of us are missing basic vitamins that boost our energy. Since we feel sluggish, we supplement our lack of energy with caffeine, creating a dependency on caffeine because we don't know how to make better choices with food.

Yes, it will be hard to wean yourself off caffeine. I used to be a two cups of coffee-a-day drinker. After quitting cold turkey, I found the habit was harder to break than the actual "need" for it. We get so used to running to coffee when we are bored or at the first sign of grogginess. Many times, afternoon sluggishness can be pushed away by walking for five to ten minutes. Even though it may seem impossible, especially when you are already struggling so much, eliminating caffeine from your diet will make a huge difference in the speed of your recovery.

Don't forget, any tea that isn't herbal will have caffeine in it. Even decaffeinated teas and coffee will have residual caffeine in them,

PRACTICAL TIPS FOR RECOVERY

so stay away from it all until you stop experiencing symptoms of anxiety/depression. Sodas and many flavored beverages, even some "waters," are infused with caffeine these days. Read labels to ensure you aren't accidentally aggravating your nervous system and instead, encouraging quick healing.

I really enjoy drinking Zevia when I am looking for a non-caffeinated sweet treat. They are all sweetened with stevia, which is much better for your nervous system and a couple of them are caffeine free. There are also a ton of herbal teas you can try until you find something you like. If you are anything like me, drinking plain water all day, every day gets boring. So, you can try Zevia's, herbal teas or experiment with infusing water with fruit so you don't feel deprived.

2. Alcohol ain't gonna fix it.

Yeah, I get to be the bearer of bad news again. If ripping your heart out by taking away caffeine wasn't bad enough, now I am coming for your booze. Before we go too far into this topic, let's address the elephant in the room first.

Are Christians allowed to drink?

Based on my study of scripture, I believe the answer is yes. Christians can drink alcohol if they choose (John 2:1-12). However, this is a topic you need to study for yourself. Don't decide to drink or not drink because I told you so. Colossians 3:17 says, "And whatever you do, whether in word or deed, do it all in the name of the Lord Jesus, giving thanks to God the Father through him."

Even though this is a hot button topic and some people may assume I am endorsing alcohol by writing this, I am not. I believe drinking is something you and Jesus need to come to an agreement about on your own. However, I know there are many people that do drink, so I want to make sure you fully understand the effects of alcohol on your body before you make that choice.

Many people drink alcohol because it calms their nerves. Since it is a depressant, it literally suppresses the nervous system and gives people the "chilled-out" feeling they may have a hard time finding on their own. The problem is that while alcohol calms you down when you drink it, it can have the opposite effect as it leaves your body. In an article titled "Should I avoid alcohol during recovery from an anxiety disorder", Jim Folk said:

> "While you might feel better while drinking alcohol because small amounts of alcohol increase GABA, the neurotransmitter primarily responsible for calming the body, higher amounts of alcohol increase cortisol, one of the body's most powerful stress hormone stimulants . . . research has shown that regular alcohol consumption can keep cortisol levels elevated during the day rather than tapering off."[9]

A big factor in why you might be cycling through anxiety and depression is over consumption of caffeine and alcohol. Ingesting large amounts of those on a daily basis basically sends your body on an emotional roller coaster. If you continue to self-medicate to deal with raging symptoms from self-medicating the day before, it will never end. You have to break the cycle at some point.

At the beginning of recovery, I did not drink alcohol at all, at least for the first six months. As time went on, I tried one glass of wine here and there. Currently, because I am on a strict diet per my doctor, I am not drinking at all. You will have to be patient with your body and allow yourself time to find a new rhythm. Let your body be free of anything and everything that could contribute to keeping it stuck. After a few months, you might be able to handle one small drink per week. By small, I mean 4 oz. of wine or a 12 oz. beer. Stay away from liquor and mixed drinks. All the added sugars in mixed drinks will amplify the symptom backlash the next day. We will talk more about sugar in the next section. Oh, joy!

Each person is different. You may not notice as much of a backlash from alcohol as you do from caffeine, though the basic principles for how alcohol affects the body are the same for everyone. It does calm your nervous system at first and can increase stress hormones after you consume it. It can also affect your blood sugar levels and cause symptom spikes if taken on an empty stomach. So, keep all these things in mind before you try to have a drink. At the end of the day, is one drink worth rebounding for an entire day? That's what you will have to decide.

3. Sugar won't make you sweeter.

Sugar is another thing you will need to limit while recovering. Foods high in sugar can put stress on the body in the same way caffeine and alcohol does. Most Americans have no idea how much sugar they consume because it's hidden in so many things. What we consider "a little sugar" is more than what we need in an entire day. We also need to define what I mean by sugar; added sugars (brown or white) are the problem. Rachel Link, registered dietician from DrAxe.com, says:

> "Contrary to popular belief, there are very few differences between brown and white sugar in terms of nutrition, and both can have detrimental effects when it comes to your health . . . Not only is sugar high in calories and carbohydrates yet lacking in important micronutrients, but sugar consumption has also been tied to a slew of negative side effects. Specifically, research shows that added sugar consumption can contribute to chronic conditions, such as heart disease, diabetes, obesity and fatty liver disease. It may also lead to weight gain and fat gain, which can **increase** the risk for many other conditions as well."[10]

Added sugars, i.e. anything that isn't naturally occurring in food, whether that is cane sugar, turbinado, artificial sweeteners like sucralose and aspartame, are not good for your body and will mess with your blood sugar and nervous system. Natural sugars found in fruit or honey are much better for you and easier to process. If you are super annoyed with all the things you "can't have" during recovery, you can try substituting white refined sugar, sucralose and aspartame with stevia, honey, or monk fruit. They won't affect your blood sugar and/or nervous system as drastically and you can still enjoy yummy treats.

According to the Dietary Guidelines for Americans 2020 - 2025, we should take in less than 10% of daily calories from sugar. On a standard 2,000-calorie diet, that equals about 50 grams of sugar per day.[11] Consider how many Americans drink one or more sodas a day. A 12 oz. soda generally has 35-40 grams of sugar in ONE CAN. So, after you've drank one soda, you can have no more sugary treats for the rest of the day. Those other 10 or so grams of sugar (and more) will likely be hiding in salad dressings, sauces, soups and other things you eat but are totally unaware contain sugar.

There's a particular restaurant that shall not be named, but is often referred to as "The Lord's Chicken," hallelujah. At said restaurant, I was shocked to find that one small packet of honey mustard dressing had fifteen grams of added sugar in it. **Fifteen grams.** So, if you are enjoying the Jesus chicken and scarf down a couple packets of honey mustard along with it, you can have an entire day's worth of sugar in one sitting. It's those types of sugars that are so damaging to the body, because we are completely unaware of how often we consume them.

While everyone understands that sweets like ice cream and candy need to be limited, most people don't understand how sweet things they eat every day are. Sorry friend, but those blended frappa-mocha-way-too-much- sugar-latte's gotta go. Sugary drinks, dipping sauces and salad dressings are some of the biggest culprits for added sugars that people are completely blind to. If you are trying to be diligent with your recovery strategies (and I hope you are), you could unintentionally be sabotaging yourself with the things you eat. So, pay attention and read labels. It will make a huge difference.

4. Volunteering

Since we spent the last three sections talking about everything you can't do, let's switch gears and talk about what you can do. You can and should find a place to volunteer. You may struggle with feelings of worthlessness. It may seem like there's no light at the end of the tunnel and you have no purpose. Even if you'd rather stay inside and alone, don't. A simple way to combat feeling purposeless is to get out and do something.

Find something you love and if you don't know what you love, try something new. You may have to step outside your comfort zone, but it doesn't have to be painful. Go to an animal shelter and play with orphaned kitties. Giving them comfort will lift your spirits and remind you that you can make a difference in the world, even when you are in pain. If animals aren't your thing, try helping the elderly at a nursing home. You could also look into mentorship programs like Big Brother, Big Sister. There are so many opportunities out there for you to make a difference.

Seeing yourself as a valuable member of society is huge! We've talked so much about changing your thinking with God's truth. What's even better is when God's Word comes alive. You may hear, "You are God's handiwork. Created in Christ Jesus to do good works" (Eph 2:10). That may seem hard to believe, but if you give your time to help others, you will see how you are more than capable of doing good works.

The times when I was teaching in middle-school ministry or volunteering at an animal shelter were a flicker of light in my usually dark days. It was mind-blowing to see how God could use me to inspire others, even though I felt anything but inspiring. If He can do it for me, He can do it for you. You just have to take the step of faith and trust God will use even the smallest act of obedience for His kingdom.

5. Naps on naps on naps

Here is another thing you can and should do during recovery. REST! Take all the naps! Please do it. Prioritize rest and sleep. Don't let anyone make you feel ashamed for resting. There's something in the American psyche that sees rest as a burden and people who "need it" as weak. It's baffling really. We look at those who take thirty minutes to pause during their day to decompress as lazy or unproductive. Yet, we forget a very important and obvious fact for why we need to do these things.

We are human!

We need rest. We don't control the world. That's part of why God instituted a Sabbath for us and why we've spent every day since the seventh day of creation fighting against it. We want to be needed. We want to be productive. We want to be useful, so much so that we chug sixteen gallons of coffee every day to prove to ourselves that we are something other than what we are, humans, not super-heroes.

Our bodies have limits, and we have to accept them. Especially while you are in recovery, it will be important to do Christian meditation or take quick power naps when you can. These things will help calm the emotional center of your brain and give the rational part of your brain more room to take the lead.

If you are struggling more with depression and finding yourself wanting to sleep all day long, I would adjust this slightly. Christian meditation, like Abide (I'll leave the website in the reference section[12]), will help calm your mind and be a great refresher mid-day. However, you need to be careful of sleeping more than eight to ten hours a day. After about ten hours, you push beyond the recommendation for extra rest. Getting too much rest will make you sluggish and can keep you stuck in a cycle of feeling like you can't leave your bedroom.

Each person is different. There is no formula, but these general guidelines are here to give you an idea of where to start. Seven to eight hours of sleep per night is best and up to ten if you are trying to heal from any kind of sickness or mental health issue.[3] As a side note, don't compare yourself to anyone else, especially people who aren't dealing with mental health recovery. You will not have the same energy levels as them, so don't expect to.

You won't be able to juggle as many things as them, and that's OK. Get comfortable with setting new, temporary limits for yourself so you can heal and get better as fast as possible. If you try to keep the same pace as others, you will wear yourself down, put unneeded stress on your body and keep yourself hyperstimulated and/or overwhelmed.

Take a nap. Meditate for 15 minutes. Go to bed early. Do whatever makes sense for your body and ask the Lord to partner with you in the process so you have help discerning what's best and when.

6. Exercise

Exercise is an important part of any lifestyle, but especially important for someone in recovery. While you may think the more exercise the better, that is not one hundred percent true when it comes to recovering from anxiety. As we talked about before, part of being hyperstimulated is due to an overload of stress hormones in your body. When you exercise, you get an immediate rush of serotonin and dopamine that gives you an euphoric feeling; many refer to it as the "runner's high." Everyone will tell you that exercise is great for fighting off depression and anxiety for that reason. They aren't wrong.

But, what people forget is, when you exercise intensely you put stress on your body. The stress of pushing your body a little further than you have before is what makes it change, but it also increases cortisol and adrenaline[13]. For the average person, an increase of these stress hormones is almost undetectable. But for a person with an anxiety disorder who is already living with an overload of "stress chemicals," the last thing you want is to add more.

Some people won't see the effects of the stress hormone increase until a day or two after the exercise. So, they may not relate the strenuous workout they did Sunday with the "random" anxiety symptom increase Monday or Tuesday. I didn't for a long time. All I ever heard was that a hard workout was a good stress relief. So, I kept at it, even though I would feel symptom increases the day of or the day after a workout.

Currently, my doctor has given me the green light to do light cardio and weight lifting only. I really wanted to train for a half marathon this year, but my doctor said my body still wasn't ready. It hasn't always been this way for me; I used to work out hard and felt great afterwards. But my body has been changed by everything I've gone through over the last six years. Your body may change too. That's OK. Listen to how your body is responding now and do what you need to so you can continue to heal.

As a general rule of thumb, daily, light to moderate exercise is best until you are not experiencing symptoms of stress. The length won't matter so much as the intensity. If you are, ahem, over thirty and really need the exercise to maintain a healthy weight, you might need to increase the length of time you walk instead of increasing the intensity. Walking, strength training and cardio are all great. Just make sure to not get your heart rate super high. That is the place you will start to put stress on your body and notice an increase in stress hormones/symptoms after a workout.

7. Praying in pairs.

This is a spiritual but practical tip I've learned and seen so much personal growth because of it. For the longest time I prayed, "Jesus, rid me of fear, doubt, despair, etc. Remove my toxic, old ways of thinking and let there be not a shred of fear in my body from here on out." That's not a bad prayer. Wanting to overcome and be rid of fear is great. But there's a spiritual principle of "binding and loosing" that many people forget. When you "bind" something evil in your life, whether it be a negative thought, evil spirit, or a bad behavior, you are ridding yourself of the evil and using your authority in Christ to change it. But you can't stop there . . . and why would you? You also need to loose the good: like trust, joy, peace, hope, etc.

Praying in pairs means that you pray for the evil to go but also for the fruit of the Spirit to come. For the longest time, I only prayed for fear to go, and I still struggled with believing that I had authority over my mind. I knew it was true, but I couldn't get past the fear and doubt. When I intentionally asked God to give me confidence and trust in His Word that I knew to be true, that's when things really changed.

I started having revelations that led to confidence. I noticed myself being less afraid of my thoughts. I found myself facing the fear with more strength. Don't be discouraged if you only see a little change at a time; that's how it was for me too. Renewing the mind is slow, painstaking work.

Asking for God's help, to give you the confidence you don't have, will bring a major increase you could never get on your own. When you see change, even if it is the slightest bit, praise Him for that! Take that little bit of growth and drink in a deep breath of hope. That is a sign things are changing. That is a sign God is working. Big changes are great; we all want the mountains moved. But don't get discouraged if the mountain is chipped away layer by layer, piece by piece. You can get excited about that, because change is still coming!

8. Stay connected to Jesus, even if you don't feel Him.

I can't tell you how many days I was afraid of reading my Bible. Many Old Testament passages and even some in the New Testament would send my overstimulated mind spiraling out of control. Some days, I would start reading, get frustrated and throw the Bible across the room. It made me so mad that the one place I was supposed to find peace became yet another place I got overwhelmed. Some days I told God to go away and leave me alone, because I wasn't sure if I could trust Him. Thankfully, He didn't listen.

Even if your mind is spinning with Scriptures that seemingly assault you. Even if it seems like Jesus is nowhere to be found. Even if your Bible appears dull and you'd rather do anything than try to decipher Leviticus again, keep reading. Keep going to church. Keep spending time with believers. I can't tell you how much I grew during the times where I felt like I was stagnant. It's impossible to explain the feeling I get when I look back at things I used to think and see how far I have come.

Don't fall for the lie that says Jesus isn't here if you don't feel Him. Don't believe He has left you for a second. If His spirit lives inside you, it is physically impossible for Him to leave you. The good news is, He wants it that way. He kind of did it on purpose, actually. So don't despair, friend. Even if Bible reading is dull right now, I promise He is planting things in you that will all come together. If you aren't connecting with sermons at church and you wonder if there's a point to going at all, there is.

I am so thankful for all those days where it felt like Bible reading and church-going was pointless. Now, I look back and see how God used me to encourage someone when I didn't know it was happening. Now, when I pray and have tons of Scripture written in my heart, I see the point to spending time in the Word, even when it feels like it accomplishes nothing. Now, I see Jesus was changing me the whole time. Now, I know Him intimately and deeply in ways I never could have if I had given up. Every word you read matters. Every time you worship matters. Every day you keep pressing in matters. Don't quit.

9. Get into counseling. Don't stop until your counselor says you're ready to.

Counseling is one of the most important things I did while I was recovering. Twice a month, every month, for two years, I saw my counselor. I still talk to him from time to time now. I don't think we ever get "over" the need for having someone to process things with. Family and friends are fine for that, but a counselor who has studied the mind and the Bible will be far more helpful in walking you toward freedom.

Earlier in the book, I mentioned a friend who said, "If you aren't 'fixed' after being with a counselor for six months, he isn't doing his job." So, I'd like to remind us all there is no formula for counseling. Everyone is different. We have all faced different levels of trauma. While one person may find significant breakthrough in six months, it may take you a year. Don't compare yourself to anyone else. **They have not lived your life.**

There is no way for you to expect to heal at the same rate as them when they haven't been through the same things as you. Please don't be the person who heaps shame on people for how long their processes take, especially if the one you are heaping shame on is yourself.

No matter how hard it was for me, something in me knew there had to be a way to overcome. Something in me kept hoping, kept believing. There was no way being a slave to fear was the life Jesus had for me. Thankfully, I let hope override my friend's comment and all the others insensitive people have thrown at me. I kept fighting because I knew a day would come that I would be sitting here writing this book. I knew God could and would use my pain and turn it into glory. And He is.

He will do the same for you. Find a Christian counselor. Let them help you. If you don't like opening up to people, you will have to ask God for help to move beyond that. Outside of a supernatural encounter, people are His chosen vessel for healing. We are His hands and feet. A Christian counselor should be a replica of how Christ would engage with you if He were sitting in front of you.

I did say "should," because I've seen enough counselors to know not all of them are. The Anxiety Centre, (see the reference page for contact information), is an amazing resource that I would recommend to anyone.[14] They are hands down the best group that deals with mental health issues. Every counselor there has walked through some sort of mental health struggle themselves, so they never teach you textbook methods without knowing the realities of how to apply them.

If you've tried a dozen counselors and still haven't found a helpful one, don't give up. In the meantime, I'd recommend reading Dr. Caroline Leaf's book, Who Switched Off My Brain.[15] It's an invaluable tool and very similar to what is taught through Anxiety Centre.

10. Get rid of the toxic.

Boundaries are hard. They are very hard for a lot of people; especially when you have to set them because someone you love is hurting you. While it may seem wrong or even "ungodly" to take space from people for a temporary amount of time, I promise you it isn't. Jesus said to forgive seventy times seven (Matt 18:22), but forgiveness doesn't mean you have to stay in a relationship with someone who doesn't respect you. In Luke 9:5, Jesus tells his disciples to shake the dust off their feet if people refuse to receive their message, figuratively displaying a removal of connection to their actions. It's as if they said, "I am wiping my hands of this now."

In Matthew 5:32, Jesus says that in the case of infidelity, divorce can be permissible. As we can see through these few scriptures, there is a place for distancing ourselves from people's unhealthy behavior. Jesus wants us to reach the broken, but His desire isn't for us to be destroyed in the process. As a good rule of thumb for recovery and for life, if you cry, end up frustrated, or feel worse about yourself the majority of the time you are with someone you love, you need to take a break from them.

Relationships are hard; there is no getting around that. However, a person who loves you won't repeatedly make you feel like you aren't loved or don't matter. That is not love (1 Cor 13:4). So, in an effort to eliminate stress while you are healing your heart and body, put some distance in unhealthy relationships.

Don't call them. Don't text them. Unfollow them so you don't see them on your social media feed. Then, just breathe. Take a breath and let it go for a while. Even if they are family. Even if they are life-long friends. Sometimes, you just need space.

It doesn't have to be forever. You can set a limit for how long you will cut off contact and then reevaluate the relationship after a few months. But whatever you do, don't guilt yourself into opening that door again until you are healthy and able to have an honest conversation about what needs to change in the relationship.

Use the time away to write down what hurt you about the relationship. Pray and ask God how to humbly present your pain to them without blaming them for everything that happened. Ask God where you went wrong in the relationship. Then, create a few healthy boundaries for what you will allow in the immediate future until things are better between the two of you.

At this point, things might get a little messy. Please understand that because you want to grow and change, it doesn't mean the other person will too. They may beg for you to be in their life. They may claim they "can't live without you," but still not want to change. If this happens after you've taken some time apart, evaluate how your frame of mind was during the time they were gone.

Were you more peaceful?

Did you grow in your relationship with Jesus more?

Did you show yourself more grace?

If the answer to these is yes, it **may** be time to let them go permanently. If we are talking about family, it can get tricky. You may have to see them at certain events. That's OK. It's completely appropriate to have relationships where you see a person only when you have to. You can love someone, be kind to them and still not have anything beyond a surface-level relationship. Sometimes, that's exactly what Jesus would do.

I know these ten tips are a lot to take in. You will probably need to re-read this chapter multiple times to absorb all the information. Don't expect yourself to get it all at once or be able to apply it all at once. Start with the top three and work on those for a few weeks. Then, when you feel confident about those steps, add in a few more. You can't do everything at once, but after you add all these things into practice and see how your life has changed, you won't regret it.

Chapter 8:
GRACE AND HONEY

"It's one of the greatest gifts you can give yourself, to forgive. Forgive everybody." -Maya Angelou

I've probably written and rewrote this book a dozen times. A decade ago, when I first started writing, this book was a scathing letter outing every person who had ever wronged me. I was hurt, I saw myself as a victim and I needed a place to right the wrongs I'd experienced in my life. My refusal to forgive led me to believe this was the only way. I felt my abusers deserved to be outed. It seemed right to let the world know who they "really were." Yet, the Bible says that "love covers a multitude of sin" (1 Pet 4:8).

It also says that "love doesn't dishonor others and keeps no record of wrongs" (1 Cor 13:5). Forgiveness is sand paper to our flesh. It's gritty and feels harsh against our open wounds, yet when applied, you'll find that it smooths out the jagged edges of a broken heart. Forgiveness is often undervalued and seen as "optional" in life. Even in the church we hear things like:

"I would forgive them but…"

"Do you know what they did to me?"

"Why would I forgive and just let them get away with it?"

And my personal favorite, "I'll forgive them when they apologize."

I used to live by the last statement. My refusal to take the first step toward forgiveness only served as a shovel that dug my pit of brokenness deeper and deeper. The Bible doesn't put stipulations on forgiveness. It doesn't say forgive if you feel like it or forgive only after they've earned your favor back. Forgiveness is so important that it was one of the things included in the prayer Jesus used to teach his followers how to pray (Matt 6:12)! In a foundational lesson on prayer, Jesus spoke about the Lord's will being done, forgiveness and temptation. If He chose those topics as the main things to focus on during prayer, then I'd say we'd better make a point to pay attention and do something with it.

What often ends up happening is forgiveness is looked at like wall decor in a guest room. It's nice if you can afford it. If your hurt wasn't "deep enough" and you have the mental/emotional wealth available to extend forgiveness, then good for you! Go for it. We think forgiveness may be a great option if you have time. If you are one of those people who can take the time to build up their spiritual muscles and forgive, that's awesome, you go Glen Coco!

If you happen to have that mentality, may I say something to you? Forgiveness is not optional, it's required (Col 3:13, Eph 4:32, Luke 17:3). Jesus doesn't leave any room for us to debate whether we should or should not forgive. Though, most of us overlook that forgiveness is not only for the person who harmed you, it is for your heart too.

Forgiveness, like wall decor, is a much more important piece in our house of healing than many may realize. Mind renewal sets the foundation for your healing and forgiveness is one of the ways you will have to learn to think differently if you want to be healthy and whole. Many people miss the blessing of forgiveness because they see it as a chore rather than a blessing. Like a gold wall sconce, forgiveness brings light and beauty to your life you may not have realized you were missing.

I'm taking an entire chapter to speak on this subject because it was one of the first things God addressed with me when I began my journey to health and wholeness. For a long time I was a very bitter person. I knew what forgiveness was but I had no clue how to apply it. I carried my burdens on my back like a trophy, instead of surrendering them, like an overbearing boulder, before the feet of Jesus.

For years, I forgave no one. I would have random outbursts of anger for no reason. There was one person in particular, who had never done anything wrong to me, who could walk in the room and send me into a rage. I think subconsciously I knew I was safe with her and my heart was so desperate for release, I unleashed on the most undeserving person. She wasn't the problem, my heart was.

I think this is partially why Jesus made such a big deal about forgiving those who hurt you. It's bad enough when someone breaks God's laws of love, but what's even worse is when we hold onto that offense and continue the cycle because we can't let go of the pain boiling inside of us. When you are hurt and you internalize pain, there are only two options for what can happen after that. You either forgive and release the pain to Jesus or you spew it onto everyone around you. The pain will have to be released somewhere. Deep heartache is too much for a person to bear. Our bodies and minds are not made to carry that kind of weight.

So, the question isn't **if** it will come out, but on **who** and **when**.

When trying to apply principles of forgiveness we can also make the mistake of thinking forgiveness means denying our feelings and sweeping them under the rug. This isn't true. For a season, as I was beginning to learn about forgiveness, when someone hurt me, I would immediately say out loud, "I forgive them. I'm over it," then I would move on like nothing happened.

I never processed how it hurt me.

I never vocalized my feelings.

I just thought, OK. *God told me to forgive, so that's what I have to do. Time to let it go, stop worrying about it and move on.*

What's interesting is, Jesus doesn't tell us to "stop talking about it and move on." In one of the most popular scriptures on forgiveness Jesus says:

"Therefore, if you are offering your gift at the altar and there remember that your brother or sister has something against you, leave your gift there in front of the altar. First go and be reconciled to them; then come and offer your gift." (Matt 5:24)

I love the way HELPS Word-Studies explains the meaning of reconciled in the original Greek. It says reconciled means "where people in conflict come together through meaningful change." When Jesus instructed people to go to their brother or sister and be reconciled, He wasn't saying pretend like you have no feelings, say your sorry and get over it. This word reconciliation shows the end goal is for us to make a meaningful change in the relationship so we can move forward.

In Lysa Terkurst's book, Good Boundaries and Goodbyes, she says:

> "We can make the choice to forgive the one who hurt us for the facts of what happened. But then we must walk through the much longer process of forgiving and healing from the impact another person's actions have had on us."

Romans 12:18 says, "If it is possible, as far as it depends on you, live at peace with everyone."

As far as it depends on you.

Make meaningful change.

These passages combined show us a picture of someone who makes every effort to live in peace with people, but doesn't rely on others to forgive. You are responsible for your own forgiveness (Col 3:13). You are responsible for processing your emotions and allowing the Lord to heal the hurt (Jer 17:14, Rom 5:1-2). Thank the Lord our peace isn't dependent on another person muttering a half hearted apology. Thank the Lord we have the ability to live free of bitterness and unforgiveness no matter what happens to us.

God has given us access to so much peace, we just have to follow His laws of love to receive it.

If we go back to the analogy of forgiveness being like home decor in our house of healing, I think we can draw out a few other important points. I know many of you ladies reading this will understand that when we decorate our home, we often do it for ourselves, but we also do it with our guests in mind, right? We add flowers to the table, decorative mirrors on the wall and candles to every surface imaginable, why?

We do it because we care about how it makes our guests feel when they walk in our home. They feel welcomed, wowed and hopefully, at peace. Decorating is a gift that we get pleasure out of, but we also enjoy doing something that will make our guests smile. While there is nothing wrong with creating a calming space for people to visit, the problem comes when we view forgiveness in a similar lens, as a gift that we withhold or release based on how we feel about another person.

They don't deserve my forgiveness, you might think.

I refuse to let them off the hook.

They need to pay for what they did!

This all seems reasonable when we are blinded by anger and bitterness, but forgiveness is not home decor. We do not get to decide how much or how little we use based on a person's behavior or our feelings about it. Hanging onto unforgiveness is the equivalent of dumping black paint on every surface of your home, inviting your friends over for a party and celebrating your "decorative genius." You just destroyed your house, yet you are living as though you have something to celebrate and worse, something to share with others.

Friend, don't be deceived. The main person you hurt with unforgiveness is **you**. Unforgiveness holds you hostage to an insult and forces you to live in perpetual awareness of what happened to you every day after. I promise you, destroying yourself with bitterness, much like destroying your own house, will hurt you just as much, if not more, than releasing the sins of another.

Forgiveness is essential if we want to live peace filled lives. God doesn't want you living in a dark, isolated place wallowing in pain from ten years ago. He wants you free, thriving and full of life. **Forgiveness is your ticket out of the past and into the future.** For so many years, I spent every day chained to what people did to me. It didn't matter the size of the offense. Once bitterness took over, any perceived slight became a reason to be mad. Every hurt was a reason to feel victimized and bind myself tighter and tighter to the hurt.

While I take full responsibility for ignoring God's Word and choosing to stay in unforgiveness, I also know that the cycle of bad behavior didn't start with me. Generation after generation of people before me continued the pattern of abuse and unforgiveness. Though, the further I go back, the longer the line of brokenness goes. In reality, it goes all the way back to Adam.

When looking back at the heartache and pain you went through, you have to remember the people who hurt you were hurt too. Everyone has probably heard the saying, "Hurt people hurt people." Yet, when we are on the receiving end of that hurt, we ask questions like, "Why would they do that?" or "How can someone be so evil?" While I won't sit here and advocate for the horrible choices people make, what I do want to say is **they were hurt too.**

People don't tear other people down because they have high self-confidence.

People don't live with unreasonable standards while, at the same time, allowing themselves the space not to be perfect.

I urge you to embrace this as you wrestle through the need for forgiveness. When thinking about the people who abused or mistreated you, remember, they were probably a victim of the same thing at one point in their lives.

People can be pretty bad at acknowledging and expressing their feelings. Most people, like I did, tend to dump their pain on those closest to them. So when we look back on those who hurt us, we have to imagine the moment they were the victims. Imagine how much they had to endure to get to a place where their hearts were so numb they could hurt people without thinking twice about it.

Don't get me wrong; we are all born with a sin nature. We are all selfish at birth. However, people who are loved well don't go around treating others like dirt. When you are loved well, you love well. You perpetuate the cycle of behaviors you are taught or endure, for better or worse.

Many of us perpetuate these cycles without realizing it. I made so many awful choices as a teen that were directly related to the pain I carried and was unable to verbalize. As a young girl, who didn't know what to do with her emotions, I learned to drown them in alcohol and attention from boys. When we make bad decisions out of a broken heart, what we need more than anything is an advocate; we need someone to fight for us. We need someone to show us the wrong, but love us anyway. **Anger and unforgiveness towards a broken person will never be a part of the solution that sets them free.** Whether that broken person is you or the person who hurt you.

So, when you look at your past, remember Jesus died to cover your sins and the sins of the person who hurt you. Don't expect grace if you don't have a heart willing to give it. Grace doesn't excuse sin; it chooses to forgive and love in spite of it.

Learning this has freed me to look at my past, and those who used to be villains in my story, with eyes of compassion. This grace doesn't only extend to others. I've had to allow the grace of God to cover the memories of my own bad choices like thick Tennessee honey. His grace consumes much in the same way honey does. When honey covers a thing, you can't look at it the same way.

GRACE AND HONEY

The sweet liquid blurs your line of sight until the pastry, or the memory you hold in your heart, is only visible through the filter of ooey, gooey goodness. Isn't this what we all need; isn't this what we all want? Isn't there a place deep down in our hearts where we think, *I know I've screwed up, but I wish someone would love me anyway.* At the very least, we wish we could love ourselves anyway. Friends, it's possible. It is absolutely possible to let God's ooey gooey goodness pour over you until you can't see yourself the way you used to.

Thankfully, as an adult, I can look back at my childhood with eyes of grace and love. I can look back at family members who made really bad choices and know they regret them as much as I regret mine. God often reminds me, when people are acting out, that they are broken little boys and girls who need to be loved by their Father. As I have pressed into the principle of forgiveness, something miraculous has happened. I have actually grown to love the people I used to hate.

This isn't a testament to how spiritual or amazing I am. It's the reality of being a believer in Christ and carrying the heart of my Father inside me. When you walk in His laws of love, you can't help but feel His love for others. You will love people you have no reason to love. You will feel deep compassion for people who don't deserve it.

When you follow Christ, your house will begin to beam with lights of forgiveness and grace. Then, you'll know God is changing you and your house will become a much more inviting place. When you forgive without question and love without reason, you can know with certainty, your heart is healing.

Chapter 9:
MASTERING THE MELODIES OF OUR HEARTS

Tears poured from my eyes as I choked out, "I'm in a really hard season." I sobbed as a roomful of blank, teenage faces stared back at me. I was the leader of a middle school church group. I was supposed to be leading them in a game that helped us get to know each other. But there I sat, sobbing uncontrollably. This was my own personal nightmare.

That moment marked a season where God dealt with a lie that kept me bound for years. Up to that point, I believed sadness was a weakness and expressing hard emotions was not something "mature" Christians did. Somewhere along the way, the enemy convinced me that bottling my feelings was for my best and the benefit of everyone around me. It wasn't until God breathed His spirit of truth into that clogged artery in my heart, that the toxic sludge of satan's lies began to loosen and years of repressed pain came pouring out.

The Psalms (and the rest of the Bible for that matter) are full of gut wrenching expressions of human pain. King David will rip your heart out, man. Even though King David slept with a married woman and had her husband murdered, he was also called a man after God's heart. Seems a little crazy, right? Why would God give a murderer such a complementary title? Even though David obviously had some character flaws, the one thing he did right was take those failures to God.

David went to God when he screwed up.

David went to God when he was scared.

David went to God when he was disappointed or angry.

MASTERING THE MELODIES OF OUR HEARTS

You don't have to try hard to see the full range of David's emotions on display in the Bible. Look at the texts below and see how vulnerable David was with the Lord.

Psalm 61 says:

> "Hear my cry, O God;
> listen to my prayer.
>
> From the ends of the earth I call to you,
> I call as my heart grows faint;
> lead me to the rock that is higher than I.
> For you have been my refuge,
> a strong tower against the foe.
>
> I long to dwell in your tent forever
> and take refuge in the shelter of your wings.
> For you, God, have heard my vows;
> you have given me the heritage of those who fear your name.
> Increase the days of the king's life,
> his years for many generations.
> May he be enthroned in God's presence forever;
> appoint your love and faithfulness to protect him.
>
> Then I will ever sing in praise of your name
> and fulfill my vows day after day."

Psalm 77:1-12 says:

> "I cried out to God for help;
> I cried out to God to hear me.
> When I was in distress, I sought the Lord;
> at night I stretched out untiring hands,
> and I would not be comforted.
>
> I remembered you, God, and I groaned;
> I meditated, and my spirit grew faint.
> You kept my eyes from closing;

House of Healing

I was too troubled to speak.
I thought about the former days,
the years of long ago;
I remembered my songs in the night.
My heart meditated and my spirit asked:

'Will the Lord reject forever?
Will he never show his favor again?
Has his unfailing love vanished forever?
Has his promise failed for all time?
Has God forgotten to be merciful?
Has he in anger withheld his compassion?'

Then I thought, 'To this I will appeal:
the years when the Most High stretched out his right hand.
I will remember the deeds of the Lord;
Yes, I will remember your miracles of long ago.
I will consider all your works
and meditate on all your mighty deeds.'"

Psalm 109:6-15 says:

"Appoint someone evil to oppose my enemy;
let an accuser stand at his right hand.
When he is tried, let him be found guilty,
and may his prayers condemn him.
May his days be few;
may another take his place of leadership.

May his children be fatherless
and his wife a widow.
May his children be wandering beggars;
may they be driven from their ruined homes.
May a creditor seize all he has;
may strangers plunder the fruits of his labor.

May no one extend kindness to him
or take pity on his fatherless children.
May his descendants be cut off,

their names blotted out from the next generation.
May the iniquity of his fathers be remembered before the
Lord;
may the sin of his mother never be blotted out.
May their sins always remain before the Lord,
that he may blot out their name from the earth."

While I can't say all of David's feelings were godly, what we do see is he has no fear in sharing his emotions with God. It's in his greatest mistakes and most agonizing moments that David runs to God and not away from Him. If you want to learn how God feels about our hard and sometimes "improper" emotions, David is a great example. Because I was so annoyed by my own emotions and vulnerability for the longest time, I didn't like reading the Psalms.

I didn't understand why David was "whining" all the time. I thought spiritual maturity was anything but what he displayed in the Psalms. It seemed more effective for me to study the "meat" of the Bible; the deep theological subjects that stimulated my mind instead of my heart. After all, the book of Jeremiah says, "The heart is deceitful above all things and beyond cure. Who can understand it?" (Jer 17:9). So, what's the point in talking about feelings and all that stuff, right? It seemed utterly useless.

Before my mental breakdown in 2017, I occasionally journaled and had been in counseling a little, so I had "some" emotional awareness. I understood we all have feelings and the inner workings of what we feel are sometimes complicated. I saw the need for other people to cry and talk about pain, but not me. I could share anger. I could share joy, but sadness was not something I felt I had the privilege of letting others see.

Yet, over the years of my recovery, God would not let this subject go. No matter how many times I ignored Him, He kept drawing me into conversation about why I hid my feelings. Why did I feel they weren't OK? Where did I get that idea? Why did I believe stuffing my feelings was a healthy way to deal with them?

House of Healing

During my "relapse" in 2021, God began to deal with it. My mind was in a dark place, anxiety symptoms raged all day long and my body felt like it was on fire most of the time. But God did something in the midst of that pain. Through that season, when I was so weak, I finally gave up and began to let people see the real me, without fear of what they might think. I cried, I screamed, I fought and I cried some more.

When I thought the darkness would swallow me whole, God never left my side. He showed me there was a place for my pain; it was in His hands. I didn't need to hide it. I didn't need to be ashamed of it. I just needed to be honest about what I felt and give it to Him. Even though my heart felt like it was cracked wide open and would never heal, I was safer than I had ever been. I was hurting, but the Healer was on the job.

Smack dab in the middle of a time where I felt so out of control, God showed me that my emotions weren't a liability, **but a strength**. Many people feel shame over their emotions, yet we are all desperate for someone to be brave enough to share the reality of their inner world. Doing so makes everyone else feel a little less alone. So, the very thing we want to hide is a critical piece in helping others find freedom.

The perfect example of this is when Jesus wept in the book of John (John 11:35). This all came to a head when Mary and Martha sent word to Jesus that their brother Lazarus was sick. Yet, instead of running to him, Jesus waited two days after hearing the news before making the trip to Bethany. He knew Lazarus would die if He waited, but before leaving for Bethany He said, "This sickness will not end in death."

We can speculate all day about what brought Jesus to tears when He finally saw Mary and Martha. Though, what we do know is Jesus had every reason for hope. He knew the end of the story wouldn't be death, yet **He still wept**. Jesus Christ, the Messiah, the One with power and authority over all, wept, even though He had assurance everything would turn out OK. Doesn't that make you feel a little less crazy? Doesn't knowing your Savior wept

MASTERING THE MELODIES OF OUR HEARTS

over the pain in the world give you a little more freedom to do so?

If Jesus wept, how much more must we then?

How much more must we grieve when things hurt and we don't know how the story will unfold?

How much more must we be open with loved ones, and God, about how we are struggling?

We don't have all the answers. Sometimes our pain stems from simply not knowing the future. Sometimes our grief comes from being in a painful situation longer than we expect. There are so many questions, worries and fears that can come up when we go through different trials. It's in those moments that we learn to trust the God who knows everything we dont. That process is hard, it's messy and it's often not fun. So, we have to come to a place where we can be honest about our feelings and allow ourselves to process them.

I think this is critical to understand if we want to be healthy, emotionally stable people. Part of learning how to lead your emotions, and not letting them lead you, is being able to accept them as they come. Learning to embrace feelings will be another important layer in your house of healing. We will never be able to live in lasting peace if we are always fighting against or ignoring our emotions.

One reason many of us try to ignore emotions is because we like control. What does control have to do with feelings you might wonder? Well, everything my dear. We are never more vulnerable than when our heart is splayed open for all to see in droplets of water across our cheeks. The person who weeps openly about something breaking their heart risks being rejected or dismissed by the people they open up too.

Uncontrollable sobbing can make you feel weak and out of control. When you release the dam of emotions hiding behind the fictitious "good" you tell people you feel everyday, you may help others feel less alone, but you also risk feeling like the "overly emotional" person no one wants to be.

So, we stuff, we ignore, we suppress, because we believe risking being perceived as emotionally unstable is far worse than emotional dishonesty. We stuff because we want to feel in control of our situation and we want others to think we are in control of our situation. Nothing irritates the flesh more than the feeling of being powerless. People will do just about anything to keep up appearances to others and to themselves.

Oddly enough, the way to regain the God-given control you have is to face the very thing you think will cause you to lose it. If we never face our feelings, we will never walk in authority over them. Authority is a simple, yet tricky concept to master. Walking in authority means accepting that you will have feelings and thoughts that come from the world, the enemy, your flesh and the Holy Spirit. From there, you look at every emotion that comes through your mind as neutral until you decide if it is true or not.

If you walk in authority you don't get angry or afraid when lies come through your mind. If you know what the truth is a lie won't shake you. A person who walks in authority doesn't let emotions lead because they know who they are and whose they are. So, they never allow a temporary feeling to control decisions that could have lasting effects on their future. Exercising authority simply means feeling what you feel, observing what you think and letting neither outweigh the power of God's spirit inside of you (Luke 10:18).

For example, let's say you start a new job. You are feeling insecure, but doing your best to keep up with the workload and expectations. Then one day, you make a mistake, a big mistake that's seen by dozens of people and you're embarrassed and frustrated. You don't know how to fix it, then a thought comes through your mind, *I'm terrible at this job. I should just quit.* Right then, you've been given a choice. You can agree, get overwhelmed and quit your new job. You can also ignore all of your emotions and think, *I'm not frustrated at all. Those feelings don't matter. I'm strong in God. I'll work hard until I fix this.* For most of my life, I responded the second way. Work, work, work. Suppress, suppress, suppress. Neither of those options reflects healthy emotional processing.

The third and best option would be to stop and journal/pray through your feelings. Ask yourself what you are feeling. Write down every thought/emotion without judging for truth; just get it all out. Then go back through and scratch off everything that isn't true. Accept that uncomfortable feelings are there, but don't allow the lies to rule you. Once you've found the truth (based on God's Word) use a few Scriptures to speak out loud over yourself until the untrue feelings pass.

Having authority in Christ is often looked at as talking a big talk and/or having the courage to go head to head with demons. While our authority does give us the ability to destroy devils, it also gives us power over the less obvious ways we can become pawns of the enemy: our thoughts and emotions.

One of the most effective ways to walk in your God given authority is to embrace your emotions and learn to lead them. You can never be manipulated by something you are a master of. Emotions are a part of being an image bearer and learning to embrace and control them will bring us to a place where we can truly live in peace.

Changing The Channel

When I was in the beginning of my anxiety disorder and still didn't understand what was happening to me, I struggled to find language to explain it to others. Most everyone can understand feeling anxiety on some level. But for me, it was next to impossible to get the average person to understand how intense the anxiety I experienced was. Analogies always help me express myself and build a bridge in difficult conversations. So, I searched for something that could accurately portray my pain.

House of Healing

No offense to goth metal music people, but "screamo music" as I call it, just isn't my thing. It grates on my nerves like nothing else. I assumed there were others who could relate to the feelings of anxiety and rage I got when l heard that type of music. So, I began to tell people that my day to day thought life was like being in a 24/7 screamo concert.

Day in and day out rage, anxiety and confusion peppered me like repetitive heavy metal beats. It was horrifying to me and I wanted nothing more than to turn the music off. There is nothing wrong with wanting a peace filled thought life. However, if you remember from chapter two, the fear and frustration we can feel towards our negative thoughts and feelings can stress our bodies even further and perpetuate the cycle of anxiety. We can turn off the music, but we just have to learn how to do it in the right way.

I like thinking of emotions as the music that sets the background in our house of healing. In my life, for far too long, I felt like the dial on my radio was stuck. I tried frantically to change that station, but the more I tried, the louder it got. It seemed like I was perpetually stuck on a station, and mindset, I didn't want to be on. But it was only when I stopped fighting and stuffing my negative thoughts/feelings that the dial unlocked and I learned I could turn it on anything I wanted.

As I've already said in this chapter, stuffing your feelings will get you nowhere. It's like when your computer freezes, yet you keep clicking the mouse every two seconds to try to force it to work. You know that wont help. In fact, you know it will make it worse. But you keep clicking, clicking, clicking because something in you wants to force the machine to work the way you want it to. In some ways, our hearts are like those technological machines.

We try to force them to forget or force them to ignore. So we stuff, stuff, stuff our emotions hoping and praying we can push through the "freeze" we experience when traumatic feelings/thoughts resurface. But friend, you and I both know, the more you click on a frozen computer, **the longer it will take for it to come back to life.** And so it is with us. Try as we might, we can't stuff forever.

MASTERING THE MELODIES OF OUR HEARTS

Eventually, our hearts will act out in peculiar ways to get our attention.

The interesting thing is that once we take a moment to pause, reflect and let the emotional processing to happen, we begin the steps towards healing. Similar to a radio or a computer, once you learn how the amazing God-made machine you carry around every-day operates, you begin to gain control over its function. If you give it, and your mind, time to process, it will come back to life. We just have to come to terms with the fact that we can't "stuff" our way to freedom. Mastering our emotions means learning to feel them, process them and accept them for what they are.

Experiences.

Feelings are simply an expression of how we are experiencing the world at that moment. They change, because we change. One day, you can be five years old, crying your eyes out because you are terrified of the clown at the circus. You may have felt afraid because he seemed big, scary and slightly creepy. Then you grow up and realize it's nothing more than a man in a costume with face paint. Your feelings changed because the way you experience the situation changed.

If for some reason those old feelings of fear come up when you see the clown as an adult, you have to decide if those feelings get to have the final say. Knowing what you know now, are you going to give that circus clown the right to scare you? Are you going to give the fear of death (talking to myself here) the authority to take your ability to fly on planes? Whatever it is, you have to mentally cup those feelings into the palm of your hand and decide if you are going to be a master over this or manipulated by it?

Our feelings change. So, we can never allow a negative thought or feeling to have the final say in our lives because **what we feel could be based on a faulty perception we haven't healed.** How silly would it be to live our lives from a place of rejection if we are unconditionally loved? You may think, *Well I'm not loved. Everyone hates me. I feel rejected because I am.*

But you aren't.

People may reject you, but God hasn't. Even if your mom, dad, siblings, friends, teachers and everyone else you know reject you, rejection isnt your identity. It is merely something you experience and can't allow to overshadow the love of Christ. Because the love of God outweighs the love of people by a gazillion pounds (the super scientific emphasis added in is my own).

We can't always control what song comes on the radio. Just like we can't control random negative feelings/thoughts that come in due to our painful experiences. Yet, when they do come, we can decide if we will continue to listen to that station or tune our "frequency" to the voice of our Father. You don't have to listen to depression, anxiety, anger or doubt forever. You just don't.

You **can** change the channel.

You **can** learn to let negative thoughts and emotions pass by.

You **can** learn to accept that weird songs will pop up on the radio every now and then. That's just a part of life.

We can't control everything we experience, but we can control how we respond to it. Eventually, after some practice, when an uncomfortable tune pops into your ear, you'll listen for a moment, not get angry or scared and tune the channel to another station, if it's a song you've heard before that doesn't bear repeating.

Even if you are young enough to wonder who still listens to a radio, sigh, I'm sure you can understand this concept. There's so many melodies to listen to in life. Sometimes we need to tune our ears to joy and sing praises to God even though we feel nothing but rage. Other times, we need to tune our ears to grief and allow the Father to mourn with us in our heartbreak.

Other times, when we hear fear and anxiety coming over the airwaves, we need to find a song that shouts confidence and trust in God and sing it at the top of our lungs. Music helps us

MASTERING THE MELODIES OF OUR HEARTS

experience the world we live in. It's a friend that can put words to our experiences. But just like our emotions, we have to decide which tune is most helpful and not allow ourselves to drown in melodies of misery.

God gave us music, like He gave us emotion, to experience life at its fullest potential. Feelings are not bad. They often amplify an already amazing experience. Even if you are in a place where the screamo music is deafening or the melancholy symphony seems to never end, it's OK. You'll hear new songs again. Your radio isn't broken. This may simply be a time to allow God in so He can help you sort through the chaos. The Bible says in John 14:27, "Peace I leave with you; my peace I give you. I do not give to you as the world gives. Do not let your hearts be troubled and do not be afraid."

Don't be afraid. Let Him show you how He can tune your ears to peace. While I know that He will bring you through, maybe for now He wants to teach you how to find joy in the midst of uncomfortable melodies. Learning how to control emotions doesn't mean you'll never feel sadness or fear again. You will. You will have to learn how to accept those moments when they come and continue walking in confidence until they leave. Part of your victory will come when you live in a place of perpetual peace. But until you reach that point, finding His peace mixed in with the hard stuff is a tune worth dancing to.

Chapter 10:
LIVING IN THE UNKNOWN

"Embrace the unexpected. The things we never saw coming often take us to the places we never imagined we could go." -Unknown

We've come to the last chapter, the last piece of the puzzle. We've covered a lot of ground so far. I hope as you have been reading, the Lord has been revealing the things you need to address and now you feel empowered to do so. Now, it is time to put the roof on your house and give you a moment to look around at the work you've done and the work you'll need to do to complete your house of healing. After all, I have given you all the "parts" you need, but completing it is up to you.

I have come alongside you as an architect of sorts. I've laid out the blueprints, shown you the way, but now it's in your hand to complete the job. You may get to this point and be filled with joy. You may have nothing but happy and hopeful thoughts about the information you've learned and how it will change your life. But, I know some of you out there are overwhelmed. I wonder if those feelings of frustration come less from thinking about your next steps and instead, stem totally from the fact that you ended up here in the first place.

How did I get here?

Why do I have to read this book and none of my friends do?

Am I really going to have to live this way for the rest of my life?

If you're having these kinds of thoughts, I get it. Trust me, I get it. I've felt that agonizing sense of disappointment looking at my new "blueprints" while the ones I planned for my life went up in smoke. No one wants this life. No one lays in the cold grass, staring at the stars, dreaming up their perfect life and envisions mental and physical health issues. But here we are.

LIVING IN THE UNKNOWN

You and I, like it or not, are in this together. We've seen the pits of despair we never wanted to see. We've seen our hopes and dreams shattered as if they were more frail than the people who created them. We've seen our fair share of pain. We never wanted to be here, but here we are.

So, what do we do now?

Do we scream, cry and kick the wind in a feeble attempt to get our former selves back? Do we curse God and give up like Job's wife recommended (Job 2:9)? Do we get bitter and lash out at everyone who isn't facing the same level of pain? The question we all have to face is this: How can we embrace the life we didn't expect to have?

I can't tell you how many times I have gone through "relapses" following a period of time where I was sure I was finally getting free. It happened in the summer of 2021, in smaller spurts in the fall of 2021 and again a few times in 2022. Every time I was hit with symptoms after a spell of being free was devastating. It's one thing to say you've been in the pit for a year. It's another to say you've been in it for six.

Over and over again as my symptoms lifted, it felt as if I was a marathon runner laying my eyes on the finish line after an agonizing uphill journey. Sure, it had been hard. Sure, I thought I'd never make it, but there I was. So, maybe you can understand the gut wrenching feeling that came when old symptoms popped up, dropping a haze over the finish line, yanking the victory from my sight.

It's like I inhaled a big, exhilarating breath at what I just accomplished, only to have every ounce knocked from my lungs. If this happens once, you pick yourself up and keep going. Maybe even when it happens twice you have the strength to keep hoping you'll finish the race soon. But what happens when what you thought was a "season" turns into a way of life? How do we handle the utter disappointment and fear of walking into the life

House of Healing

we never wanted with no idea if this part of the story will be a chapter or the second half of the book?

It's heartbreaking. Let me tell you. This is where you really need to grab a hold of the principles we talked about on feelings. You need to weep. You need to mourn. You need to get raw and honest with God about your disappointment. Then, you need to decide that those feelings won't dictate your next steps and cry out to God again for trust to believe in His plan.

As I am writing this chapter of the book, I am also eye balls deep into the show *Virgin River*. Man, the people in that town go through a lot. While the lives of every townsperson looks more like *Lemony Snicket's A Series of Unfortunate Events* than real life, the tragedy the main character Mel goes through is where I want to focus. Mel has it rough from the second we met her. She loses a baby during birth and her husband dies in a car accident not too long after.

The first season is mostly about Mel struggling to accept her new life in Virgin River and trying to find her path in the story she never wanted. It's heartbreaking to see the agony this woman goes through. While I can't relate to the pain of losing a child or spouse, I can relate to being totally disoriented by life's disappointments. As the show continues, Mel begins to fall for a guy in town. He's cute, thoughtful and everything she could want, but he isn't her deceased husband. As much as he may give her butterflies, those fluttery feelings dissipate every time a memory of her late husband reappears.

What's a girl to do? What are any of us to do?

I'm sure every person reading this book has faced disappointment. I'm sure many of you understand what it feels like to have your hopes and dreams only alive in your memories. If we get stuck there, like Mel does, and like I have, we may miss the life we could have because we can't move beyond the one we wanted.

LIVING IN THE UNKNOWN

Don't get me wrong. I know some of you reading this are drowning in grief from losing a loved one. You may think, *How do I just get over him/her? How do I move beyond the life I thought we'd build?*

In no way am I diminishing the value of the person you are missing. You don't "get over" them. You don't "get over" a tragic accident that leaves someone handicapped for the rest of their life. You don't "get over" waking up one day with soul crushing anxiety that takes years to get rid of. You just don't. But what we have to try to do is release the life we thought we would have and embrace the life sitting right in front of us.

Part of what makes life so disorienting sometimes is the unknown. If God told us exactly what would happen, when it would happen and the results of it, wouldn't that make hard times so much easier? Wouldn't that keep us from doubting His goodness and love for us? We would never doubt if we had all the answers. We may not like all the things God allowed on our timeline, but we would know that things would turn out OK and this "season" wouldn't be our forever.

As much as I hate saying this, if God did things that way, He would completely remove the opportunity for us to have faith. **We would never have a chance to trust in God if the unknown was taken out of the picture.** The unknown is where we have to make the choice to believe what God's word says. The unknown is where we have to decide if we will believe our feelings or God. The unknown is where we have to look at our circumstances and the heart of our Father and declare, "This is a mess, but this isn't the end. My God can and will do more than I can imagine with this."

If we knew exactly how everything would turn out, **we** would be in control, **not God**.

Though I have hated how long my healing journey has lingered on, the roots of my faith grew deeper and deeper the longer the storm raged around me. With every whip of the wind, my heart lunged deeper into the soil of His presence, longing for a firm foundation to cling to. Yes, the storm has hurt, but it has strengthened me too. The days where it is easy and you almost forget you need God are not the days your spiritual muscles grow. Celebrating God's goodness and blessing is a good practice, but praising God when you feel good vs praising God when you're on your tenth symptom relapse is another story.

The days I wasn't sure how I was going to make it another step are when I realized God was able to carry me. I'm sure most of you have heard people say, "The Lord will give me strength," when they are facing a hard situation. Maybe that sounds nice, but maybe you aren't sure what that means or if it's a real thing that's available to you. Well friend, let me tell you, the strength of God isn't a mystical idea, it is a tangible reality He longs for you to experience. But, you have to experience weakness to appreciate His strength.

I've had more days than I have hairs on my head where I was exhausted before I ever rolled out of bed. The thought of opening my eyelids after not sleeping all night seemed impossible. Yet, I did my ugliest roll onto the carpet beside my bed, fell on my face and cried. I said, "God you have to help me. I have nothing left to give and I have an entire day to face. I need YOUR strength. Your Word says you never run out and have more than enough to give. Give me your strength God" (Ps 24:7-8, 2 Chron 20:6, Ex 15:6). And guess what? All eight jillion times I asked, He did just that.

God can give you the joy you don't have (Rom 15:13).

He can give you strength your mental/physical symptoms have zapped (Is 40:28-31).

He can give you hope when it seems illogical to hope things will get better (Rom 15:13).

All of this can only happen when we step into the unknown; when we embrace the life we have instead of the life we planned for ourselves. Only in the places where we are faced with our weakness do we realize just how strong God is. By no means am I saying that God causes all the chaos in life to teach you a spiritual lesson about Himself. If you think back to chapter three, you'll remember sin and the consequences thereof were not God's idea. But, God does use all things for good (Rom 8:28).

So, when we have these moments of heart shattering disappointment or we are facing a season full of pain, this is a moment where we have a huge decision to make. Are we going to trust God or are we not? Are we going to believe in God's goodness only on the days we feel good or are we going to believe it is a reality no matter how we feel? Are we going to step into a season full of uncertainty and heartache with a face set like flint on God's promises?

God's desire is for our healing (Matt 8:14-17).

God's desire is for our wholeness and peace (Is 53:5).

God's desire is that we walk in freedom (John 8:36).

His desire for our healing and health doesn't change because our story didn't turn out like we planned. His plan has always been the same. Redeem the people He lost. Everything about the great story of the Bible is centered on God radically loving people and doing everything in His power to bring them into wholeness, health and a perfect, loving relationship with Him again.

It's in His presence we find the fullness of joy.

It's in His heart we find our greatest desires.

It's in His hands we find the healing and peace our soul longs for.

He is it.

If you are looking at your story and wondering why it turned out the way it did, there's an even bigger reality you need to hold onto. Even though your life plan changed, God never did. He is the steadiness you need when your world turns upside down. He

House of Healing

is the strength you need when you can't move another inch. He is the light guiding you through the dark valley you aren't sure you will ever find your way out of. It's Him. He is the fulfillment of the best story we could ever write for ourselves.

I can't tell you when or how things will work out for you. I promise you, I would bang down heaven's door every second of the day if I thought God would give me that kind of insight. I want nothing more than to leave you with a blueprint that has every "t" crossed and every "i" dotted, but that's not my job.

There may be a few rooms on your blueprint that are hazy and unclear right now. Some of my "why's" and "when's" still are. You may not know what the next six months will look like . . . and that's OK. I am only here to give you a framework. God's job is to help you build the house. He is the Master Architect. He is ultimately responsible for your healing, not me. I can't fill in every detail of every day going forward, but if you follow the guidelines in this book and cling to God's book, step by step, day by day, embracing your new path will seem a little less scary.

Embrace this season of life and all you can get out of it. Don't wait until you feel better to live. Don't wait until you know things are on the up turn before you find purpose in the pain. Let people into the suck while you sit in it. Let God's grace wash over you and flow onto them. Let your heart break wide open and the pieces fall where they may.

Then, give the Master Architect the freedom to pick them up. Let Him into the rubble and watch as He begins, brick by brick, layer by layer to use the ashes to build something new. It may not be what you expect. It may not be what you want at first, but trust me, it will be everything you need. God's plans are bigger and grander than our wildest dreams.

In revealing the plan He had for my life, He gave me a vision for yours too. Day after day, I fought for healing. Day after day, we took the ashes of my pain and molded it into something strong and durable that could sustain new life. As I began to rebuild my

LIVING IN THE UNKNOWN

house with the Lord, I noticed so many others still stuck in the rubble. Sitting, waiting and hoping something could change, but not sure that it ever would. Then the Lord whispered into my ear, "Your house doesn't have to be done to help them. Go . . . tell them I will come and rebuild with them."

In the same way this book is a catalyst for your healing, your freedom can begin the healing process for someone else. But you will have to fight. You will have to go through the unknown, the hard and the scary. You will have to face everything that binds you. Because one day, after you've pushed through the rubble and began to rebuild, the Lord will tenderly grab your hand.

He'll turn you from your house and shift your gaze to the road behind you . . . and there you will see them. In the spaces where old, worn and weary houses used to be, the hurting and broken will sit. With tears in their eyes, they'll run their fingers through the ashes of what they used to call home. Everything they knew, now sits shattered before them. Much like you and I used to, they look at the mess without the hope that something beautiful could come out of it.

On that day, you'll walk down the street and plop right down in the dirt beside them. From your back pocket, you'll pull out your blueprint built with the plans and promises of the Lord. Then grabbing their hand you'll say, "Not too long ago, I was sitting right where you are." With tears in your eyes, you'll point to the picture of your house and continue, "You see this house? You can have one just like it. Where you are now doesn't have to be your forever."

Then helping them up, you will walk up the road toward your house and introduce them to The Architect. There, you'll show them the work Jesus has done on your house. Looking at the steady frame and firm foundation, hope will spring up in their eyes. In this moment, they may ask, "What is this place? Can I really have one just like it?"

Wiping the sweat from His brow, Jesus will reveal a blank piece of paper in His hand. Smiling at you and your new friend He will say, "Yes. I'm glad you asked. You can have a place like this too. It's time for you to build your very own house of healing."

So, you want to become a child of God?

Let me start by saying thank you. Thank you for giving me the privilege of having this conversation with you. I so wish I could be there, sitting right next to you, holding a hot cup of tea as we talk about the Great Creator and Lover of our Souls. He is everything and it is my honor to tell you why.

God made this world with the best of intentions. As you read through Genesis 1 and 2, you'll see that after everything He made, He said it was good. It was so good that man walked freely, side by side with God, in the midst of the beautiful garden He created for them to live in. What's even better is that they were fully naked and had zero shame. Can you imagine that? Living in a world with no shame, no relational strife, no pain and no sorrow. It had to be the epitome of perfection.

Sadly, it didn't last long. Adam and Eve were deceived, did the one thing God told them not to do and brought the curse of sin and death into the world. Before you get too mad at them, we have to remember we probably wouldn't have done much better if we were in their shoes. But God knew that before He created us. He knew we would run from Him. He knew we would rebel. He knew this world would go through destruction and chaos, yet He still created us.

More than anything in this world, God desires a loving relationship. He desires family. You can see it in the heavenlies through how God interacts with angels. He doesn't need them, but He chooses to work with them and be in relationship with them. That is who He is. So, it should be no surprise to us that the same day Adam and Eve rebelled, God issued notice to the "serpent" who deceived them. He already had a plan to redeem His creation.

The plan, simply put, was Jesus.

In the Old Testament, God lays out a system of animal sacrifices to pay the penalty for sin. He declares that "Life is in the blood and it is only through blood that one can reconcile a damaged life." (My paraphrasing - Lev 17:11). It doesn't take long for people to realize there aren't enough animals in the world to cover the cost of their bad choices. So, God sends Jesus into the world to make the one time, permanent sacrifice of life for all mankind. Jesus died in our place. He took the punishment for us and paid the penalty we never could.

For a sacrifice to take sins away, it had to be perfect. Otherwise it was just as bad as the sinner and could do nothing to help the person in need. This is why Jesus' life, death and resurrection were so miraculous. He lived a sinless life, but was tempted in all the ways we are so He could be the perfect sacrifice for us and also be a High Priest who can empathize with our struggles. His resurrection showed every spirit and human that not only was the debt paid in full, but He had power over death itself.
And because of that . . . we are free!

Today, if you are reading this and wonder what that freedom might be like, you can have it. You don't have to wonder how to get rid of the guilt of your sins. Jesus already did it. You just need to believe in Him. You don't have to go to seminary school first. You don't have to get yourself together before giving your life to God. The Bible says this, "If you declare with your mouth, 'Jesus is Lord,' and believe in your heart that God raised him from the dead, you will be saved" (Rom 10:9). It's that simple. Believe and receive.

If you want to do that right now I can walk you through a simple prayer to solidify the decision you are making. Say out loud, "Jesus, I believe you are Lord. I believe you created me, died for me and rose to conquer sin and death in a way I never could. I turn from my sin and turn to you. Thank you Jesus for saving me. Thank you for making me new."

If you just prayed that prayer . . . CONGRATULATIONS and WOO HOO! I'm so excited for you, my new brother or sister in Christ. Welcome to the family! Now, it's time for you to find a bible-believing, Jesus loving church to get plugged into so other Christians can help you walk out your new found faith. If you want, sign your name on the page below with today's date. Etch your decision in ink so you never have to doubt what you did and what God did in you because of it.

REFERENCES

1. Mackie, Tim, and Jon Collins. 2020. "Watch: Peace (Shalom) Advent Word Study Video I BibleProject™." The Bible Project. https://bibleproject.com/explore/video/shalom-peace/.

2. Folk, Jim. 2021. "Are There Good And Bad Stress Hormones?" AnxietyCentre.com. https://www.anxietycentre.com/faq/are-there-good-and-bad-stress-hormones/

3. Axe, Josh. 2022. "Researchers Try to Nail Down Ideal Amount of Sleep." https://draxe.com/health/ideal-amount-of-sleep/.

4. Leaf, Dr. Caroline. 2018. "Podcast Episode #52: What is the mind/brain connection?" YouTube. https://www.youtube.com/watch?v=I5fWL7ccaE4

5. Whitwer, Glynnis. 2017 "Finding Faith in the Dark." Proverbs 31 Ministries https://proverbs31.org/read/devotions/full-post/2017/04/14/finding-faith-in-the-dark. Accessed 27 February 2023

6. Prince, Joseph. "Guard What Comes through Your Eye- and Ear-Gates." JosephPrince.com. https://www.josephprince.com/meditate-devo/guard-what-comes-through-your-eye-and-ear-gates

7. Folk, Jim. 2021. "Caffeine And Anxiety - AnxietyCentre.com." Anxiety Centre. https://www.anxietycentre.com/faq/caffeine-and-anxiety/

8. FDA. 2018. "Spilling the Beans: How Much Caffeine is Too Much?" FDA. https://www.fda.gov/consumers/consumer-updates/spilling-beans-how-much-caffeine-too-much

9. Folk, Jim. 2022. "Should I Avoid Alcohol During Recovery From Anxiety Disorder And Hyperstimulation?" Anxiety Centre. https://www.anxietycentre.com/faq/alcohol-during-recovery/

10. Link, Rachael. 2020. "Brown Sugar vs. White Sugar, Plus 5 Healthier Substitutes." Dr. Axe. https://draxe.com/nutrition/brown-sugar/

11. USDA. 2020. "2020-2025." Dietary Guidelines for Americans. https://www.dietaryguidelines.gov/sites/default/files/2020-12/Dietary_Guidelines_for_Americans_2020-2025.pdf#page=31

12. From Chapter 7, "Practical Tips for Recovery:" https://abide.co/
Anxiety Centre. 2022. "Why do you recommend avoiding rigorous exercise?" YouTube. https://www.youtube.com/watch?v=LyFatADU8vU

13. From Chapter 7, "Practical Tips for Recovery," Anxiety Centre website: https://www.anxietycentre.com/

14. Leaf, Caroline. 2009. "Who Switched Off My Brain? Controlling Toxic Thoughts and Emotions." Amazon, https://www.amazon.com

Made in the USA
Las Vegas, NV
11 June 2024